Christmas '08

To   j

G000068922

already!

READING THE GREEN

from The Brady Bunch
x

First published in 2008 by
CURRACH PRESS
55A Spruce Avenue, Stillorgan Industrial Park, Blackrock, Co. Dublin
www.currach.ie
1 3 5 4 2
Front cover illustration by John Ireland
Cover design and typography by Bluett
Origination by Currach Press
Printed in Ireland by ColourBooks, Baldoyle Industrial Estate, Dublin 13
ISBN: 978-1-85607-975-4

READING THE GREEN

THE INSIDE LINE ON THE IRISH IN THE RYDER CUP

PJ BROWNE

CURRACH PRESS

To the Irish Ryder Cup players

ACKNOWLEDGEMENTS

It would be impossible to name all the people who have contributed to this book, wittingly or unwittingly. Apart from a few notable exceptions, a general thank-you will have to suffice.

I started following the PGA Tour in the mid-1990s. Prior to that, I was a lover of the big ball – football, rugby – and eked out a living coaching American high-school and college teams in the fundamentals of soccer. Having a UEFA licence meant nothing in Yankee land, and when the USSF refused to insure me, I turned to the small ball.

The financial remuneration from the small ball was little enough but the friendships and goodwill were greater and the intelligence factor was considerably higher. The vast majority of professional golfers in Ireland, Europe and the US are courteous and obliging. It is uncommon for a phone call not to be returned, and that includes Tiger Woods (well, he was ten years younger then and it's not possible now to contact him in the old-fashioned way).

David Feherty has been there through all of it. He hinted once that he might adopt me; fortunately he didn't. He has a beautiful daughter, Erin Torrance, and we all know where Erin got her looks from. When I first saw David's wife Anita, I thought she was his daughter.

We have many things in common. David suffered greatly when he endured a dark period of clinical depression. His honesty in writing and talking about this illness is to be admired. He knows that effective help is available and wishes to see an end to the stigma associated with mental illness and depression.

We are on an equal footing these days. He no longer plays golf and I never played it. His knowledge of the game is comprehensive.

Attend any of his clinics and that is quickly borne out. And it's true what they say about him: he is spontaneous and funny. As well as that he appreciates a well-crafted sentence, poetry and a variety of good literature. Thanks, Deej.

A special thanks to Peter Alliss and Jack Nicklaus; also to Ken Carpenter of TheGolfGazette.com, Neil Amdur, former Sports Editor of *The New York Times* and Rex Hoggard of *Golfweek* (USA).

Two friends in Ireland must be mentioned. Sean Ryan of the *Sunday Independent* has been supportive down through the years. Sean wrote the definitive book on Irish soccer, *Boys in Green*. He has a keen interest in golf and I hope his game has improved. The late Brendan McKenna, PRO, Football Association of Ireland, was a special friend and valued a good book. I treasure his hand-written letters. Brendan left us far too soon.

Dave Hannigan, the best soccer writer in Ireland and the UK, got me started in sportswriting. He has written quite a few books and is now concentrating on a lecturing career. Dave is from Cork City and a graduate of UCC: solid credentials. Dave boy, thanks.

Thanks to: Brian Keogh, sports writer; Peter Masters of *Golf World* (UK); Declan O'Donoghue of *Backspin*; Greg Francis of *Golf Ireland*; Tony Leane and Declan Colley of the *Irish Examiner*; Mark Jones of the *Sunday Tribune*; Tom English of *The Sunday Times*; and Adamhnán O'Sullivan, former Sports Editor of the *Sunday Independent*.

Finally, thanks to Currach Press for publishing this book.

PJ Browne
Springfield, New Jersey
October 2008

CONTENTS

Foreword

David Feherty

I have written a few forewords to golf books in my time but this may well be my last. I would prefer to call this a forewarning, as the author is clearly stalking me. I should really say what I like and dislike, perhaps get vindictive and settle a few old scores but no – the bastards know who they are and I am recuperating from a banjaxed elbow and haven't the energy for a fight.

I was on my bike and got into a tangle with a truck and the truck won. The writer of this book was very consoling. 'Sure can't you see and smell like a dog and you haven't lost your voice,' says he. 'You shoulda stayed with the running, pal.' You can tell I have great friends. I quit running many years ago when my ex-wife's lawyers stopped chasing me; it's taken nearly twenty years to get away.

Because my elbow is impaired I want to talk about sex. That's right; it's not a misprint. I want to talk about sex and golf and the Ryder Cup. I have read far too much about God and golf and divine design. You can find it in any coffee-table book: 'If God were going to play golf he would definitely pick...as his home course.' I say bollox to that.

For non-believers like myself God has no place in the game. I suspect that the writer of this book feels the same way. He once said to me in a rare moment of insight: 'We don't have to be religious to be moral any more than we have to believe in God to be good.' If you find a connection between these disparate subjects keep it to yourself. Where was I?

Oh yes…

The Ryder Cup is nearly as old as sex but not quite. Put the Irish in the mix and it's a different story. There was no sex in Ireland for much of the last century. There was more pressure than penetration. The same tendency attached itself to the Ryder Cup. The swinging sixties ushered in the sexual revolution and in the seventies Britain and Ireland embraced the Europeans.

Ah, the pleasures of sexual liberation and the dropping of inhibitions quicker than Moll Flanders's knickers. Maybe it was the infusion of Mediterranean, Germanic and Nordic blood. The Ryder Cup became a real contest and in a sweet role-reversal (I'm biased) the Europeans began to win Sam Ryder's trophy with pleasing regularity on both sides of the pond.

Let me tell you about Jimmy Demaret, an American Ryder Cup player. Jimmy was a flamboyant character and had a perfect record in Ryder Cup competition. My only problem with him is that he beat Fred Daly, my mentor and hero, in Ryder Cup play. Jimmy won thirty-one times on the PGA Tour at a time when prize money was low-fat, spare to non-existent. He also won three Masters so he is in elite company.

Jimmy was a great man to make a buck and played with the likes of Bob Hope and Bing Crosby. Safe to say he picked their pockets on the course, while he used his good singing voice as a nightclub singer away from the game. He was quick-witted and gregarious, with hideous taste in clothing.

Not only was Jimmy one hell of a golfer, he knew a fair bit about sex. Jimmy and sex were just about synonymous. I used to think that he invented it. You might say he put the ride in Ryder Cup. Here are some of his oft-quoted words of wisdom: 'Golf and sex are about the only things you can have fun doing without being any good at.'

I would go a little further and say that this doesn't mean you ought to stop trying to get better at both.

I believe all the facts in this book are the result of my friend's endeavour. All the bullshit is mine, even if some of it is true. I tell you one thing, though. Making the Ryder Cup team was the greatest achievement of my career and we lost. But no one can steal those memories from me. I'm certain that Smythy would say exactly the same thing. Professional golfers have always been among the few athletes who are compensated in direct proportion to how well they play but in this event they aren't paid at all and therein, perhaps, lies the reason for the event's success. Never mind the negative spin that surfaced before Brookline. It was always about a lot more than money.

Ryder Cup players are paid enough to cover expenses. The US team is permitted to nominate a charity of their choice. The Ryder Cup has always inspired antics from the competitors that they would never consider in other events. Because there is no money involved and a hell of a lot of national pride at stake, no player wants to be either a national hero or a derided goat. This is why normally self-respecting professional golfers descend to a level of gamesmanship that would not be tolerated on the professional Tours.

The Cup also inspires great courage and great character. The Americans have missed out somewhat in this area through the years. They go week to week on their own planes or travelling alone, eating alone and staying alone.

The Europeans still drive to some events and maybe even room with someone else. Some have been doing this since their amateur days. They might rent a car together or hop on a train from one event to the next. The Swedes tend to travel together and there are groups that live together for the greater part of the year.

We had a ball on the European Tour in those early days. We actually played golf in between the extra-curricular activities. It was OK to drink a lot; for some of us it was the norm. Remember we weren't making big prize money so if there was drink going (courtesy of a kind sponsor or those handy little mini-bars in hotel rooms) we were chasing.

One tends to recall the laughter and the harmless high jinks. Smythy and his wife, Vicky, were great company on the Tour, the life and soul of many a party. Now we are middle-aged, perhaps not quite grown-up, and the drinking has all but disappeared. Mind you, the Ryder Cup allows players to drink with impunity through the laughter or the tears. There are gaps, lost weekends, sometimes lost weeks and escapades that others remind you about. I must have missed out on a helluva lot of fun because I don't remember certain parties, hotels, celebrations. I did lose a trophy once after winning the Scottish Open – thanks to Led Zeppelin – but that's another story.

The Europeans are more at ease with one another, so that coming together as a team is routine. Everything outside the game is different for the Europeans and it's how these outside things affect you inside that determines whether or not you are any good at team competition.

When you look at the American players who make these teams, their personalities as competitors inevitably change a little bit. No matter how you tweak this, it still changes the way you look at someone. In Ryder Cup play, you get to know the player but you also get to know the individual because of the environment. You're thrown together with people you might not ordinarily choose to be with.

Ryder Cup matches (and in recent years the President's Cup) are the only times players abandon their individuality to play together as a unit. For fifty-one weeks they are individuals, millionaire entrepreneurs playing a solitary sport. The fifty-second week they are partners, team-mates, playing for pride and country, hoping they won't be the ones to let the team down. This is the perennial dichotomy facing the Americans and the successful captain understands what it takes to overcome it.

Even that does not guarantee success, as you will see in these pages. The Europeans have simply outplayed the Americans in recent matches. Mind you, I am still a little surprised when the Europeans win. Maybe that's a legacy from the earlier days of the Cup. The European Tour is now heavily laden with talented players and there are more and more coming through all the time. It is very satisfying to see the Irish boys doing the business for the European team.

I anticipated three Irish making the team this year. I thought Harrington and Clarky would surely be there again. I was hoping to see McGinley make it too although I knew he would have to play his way on to this team. It was great that McDowell made it as the quest for places is ultra-competitive. He should have qualified for the 2006 team as well.

Is there a golf fan anywhere who wouldn't like have liked to see young McIlroy on the team? He seems a safe bet for the future. If the youngster had made it this year he would have been the big Ryder Cup story. That could only have been positive. To have a young Irish superstar on the team would have needed no embellishment from this old boy. McIlroy's from Ulster too. Must be something in the air there.

Last (and possibly least), a few notes about the writer of this book. He claims to have discovered me in 1997, just about the time the golf world discovered Tiger Woods. Through the years, the story changed; he discovered me and I discovered Tiger. Go figure. He's got bags of balls. Who else would call Tiger Woods in Australia during the President's Cup and leave a message for Tiger to call him back. Inexplicably, Tiger did return that call. Later I found out that the message was that 'Feherty said it was okay.'

He is uniquely qualified to write about golf. He doesn't play golf and claims to know nothing about the game. That's a big plus. He looks at a golf course as a place to train and run. If there are hills so much the better. His ambition is to run barefoot in Augusta. It won't happen unless I want to lose my job with CBS.

He likes Spike Milligan and writes poetry. Another plus. Here's a guy who sat next to Paddy Kavanagh on that bench by the canal. Peej was well under the influence and offered Kavanagh a swig from his bottle. When he got no reply he got humpy and threw a punch. Next morning he awoke with a broken hand, a head full of bird shit and a desire to abandon the bottle. Punching a statue will do that to a man.

When he met Ernie Els at Westchester the talk was about rugby. Ernie, being a generous soul, offered him a beer and he drained the pitcher. Ernie looked at him wide-eyed and ordered two more pitchers. It got better (or worse) when he approached Bernhard Langer, who was alone on the putting green.

Bernhard was going through the yips at the time and they were having an intense conversation. Peej looked like he knew what he was on about and then I heard him tell the German, 'Bernhard, don't forget now, you have to langer it into the hole.' Munster rugby followers will appreciate that, more specifically those from Cork.

I have changed the locks on my door, changed my cellphone number numerous times and even moved house because of Peej. But when the time comes for my biography to be written, I want him to write it.

Texas, August 2008

INTRODUCTION

DES SMYTH AND THE RYDER CUP

Des Smyth's contribution to the Ryder Cup is detailed elsewhere in this book. He is regarded as one of the truly nice guys in professional golf and has been generous with his comments and insights for more than ten years. When I suggested dedicating this book to him, on the basis that he was vice-captain of the Europeans in 2006, he was aghast. 'I'm not deserving of it and it wouldn't be my style,' he said. 'Why don't you dedicate it to all the Irish players,' he suggested.

When Des claimed the winner's medal at the Q School for the Champions Tour, he gained immediate respect among his peers in America. They understood the commitment that he made coming off an accomplished career on the European Tour. He didn't need to take on this formidable challenge; he wanted to test himself against the world's best in the over-fifty bracket.

Smyth has always played the game on his own terms and he took a risk by entering the highly competitive Q School in the States. His longevity on the European Tour meant nothing in the US. He was equal to the challenge and after a period of adjustment to the travel and courses he was quite successful.

One of his concerns in 2002 was being away from his family for extended spells. There was also the significant matter of his daughter Karen's education; she was beginning university that autumn. These are sensitive times in any family. Fortunately, Des had the unstinting support of his wife Vicky and his children.

Six years on and Karen has graduated from university and is now employed by the HSE. Smythy has done well on the Champions Tour and in Seniors events in Europe.

This season he is not playing to his accustomed standards, the standards that would be necessary for him to stay on the Champions Tour. This will be his final season. Smyth doesn't phase his way out; when the game isn't there he moves on. In this case it will be a return to the European Tour and more time in Ireland. Des is a sportsman with a strong interest in rugby, soccer, Gaelic games and horse-racing. He took great delight in Munster's 2008 Heineken Cup win, coming as it did on the back of Ireland's disappointing World Cup performances. Des Smyth was more than happy to accept a role as vice-captain to Ian Woosnam in 2006.

> It's still a tremendous honour. Every effort was made to have an Irish captain but I'd say the decision on the selection of captain was made a long time before. Of course it would have been brilliant to have an Irish captain, whether it was Eamonn [Darcy], Christy Jr or myself. We got the next-best thing and there's no point in dwelling on the 'what-ifs'.
>
> The Ryder Cup is always a great occasion. For all the Irish players certainly, there is a strong sense that your career is not complete unless you have played Ryder Cup. I played on the first European team [1979] and also two years later. It was a dream come true for me playing against my heroes Jack Nicklaus and Tom Watson in 1981.
>
> This was Jack's last appearance as a player. Jose Maria Canizares and myself were beaten 3 and 2. Even though we played great, Jack and Tom played brilliant and the result was deceiving really. The 1981 American team was a team of all-stars – you had legends in Jack Nicklaus and Tom Watson; Hale Irwin, Ben Crenshaw, Johnny Miller, Lee Trevino, Raymond Floyd, Larry Nelson – all multiple winners on the PGA Tour and with several Major wins among them. This was golf's version of the 'dream team'.

David Feherty adds:

> I'd like to have seen Des as captain in Ireland, although Woosie was an excellent choice. I never saw Des look unhappy and he's immensely kind-hearted. He held his card for all those years and he had a great short game. I'm glad he was on our side because he was one of the most competitive players I knew. He's got a great head on him and what matters most, I think, was his ability to close the deal when he got a chance to win. Finishing the job is what separates the good players and the great ones and I'm not so sure you can coach that. I think Des provided an edge that the Americans didn't have.

Smyth has no misgivings about the future of the Ryder Cup.

> I've heard it said that if the Americans lost again in Valhalla the Ryder Cup would be in jeopardy. I don't agree with this argument at all. Okay we had beaten them three times in a row but I was still hoping we'd trounce them again this year.

Earlier in the year, he saw Harrington and Clarke making the team and Graeme McDowell 'looking good':

> Rory McIlroy is one for the future. It seems like he has been groomed for this arena. It would be great foe Irish golf to have a young superstar akin to Sergio Garcia. It's not that easy when you take your game on the road.
>
> His record to this point is very impressive and I have read strong positive assessments of him.

The Irish have contributed several key moments to the Ryder Cup and Smyth explains why:

> It goes back to the days when Fred Daly, Christy Sr and Harry Bradshaw were out there doing it. They established a tradition, a pattern of delivering in clutch situations.
>
> We would have been very much aware of that coming through and you could always go to these guys for advice. They wanted us to succeed. And you can't overlook the role played by the GUI and the Irish PGA. Our lads are very capable in all matchplay combinations. The strength and quality of the amateur game in Ireland provide a solid platform for would-be professional players.
>
> The European Tour has gone from strength to strength. I'm not certain that the Americans understand the implications of this. There's an awful lot of talented players throughout Europe and each country has a stake in the Ryder Cup.
>
> While it is gratifying to see a succession of Irish wins on the European Tour this year. We shouldn't become complacent about the ease of making future Ryder Cup teams. We have been phenomenally successful for the last ten years or so. The Irish boys will have to be at their best in the years to come and I've no doubt they will.

Smyth is not overly confident of seeing an Irish Ryder Cup captain, even in 2010.

> There are so many players in Europe who would be worthy captains. Colin Montgomerie, Jose Maria Olazabal and Sandy Lyle are just a few who come to mind. Our current big three, Darren, Padraig and Paul,

are eminently qualified to be selected as captains. Any of those three would do a superb job but there are so many others with equal merit. At the end of the day there can only be one captain. I'd like to think that we will see an Irish captain some time in the future.

1

FROM HUMBLE ORIGINS
TO GLOBAL REACH

On 26 April 1926, *The Times* of London reported:

> Mr S. Ryder, of St Albans, has presented a trophy for annual competition between teams of British and American professionals. The first match for the trophy is to take place at Wentworth on June 4 and 5. The matches will be controlled by the British Professional Golfers' Association but the details are not yet decided.

Ryder became a significant benefactor of professional golf in Britain, sponsoring numerous tournaments and attending all the major events. The wealthy seed merchant donated the gold trophy – the one we now call the Ryder Cup – insisting that it be crowned with the figure of a man putting. The trophy cost £250 and was made by the firm of Mappin and Webb. It stands seventeen inches high, weighs four pounds and is stamped with the date '1927'.

In May 1926, the British magazine *Golf Monthly* reported that a 'Walker Cup for professionals' was being arranged and that Ryder had presented a trophy 'for a contest between the two nations to be played alternately in this country and in the US at the time of the Open Championship in the respective countries'.

The outcome of the first match was a comprehensive win for the British. There was much debate about the make-up of the US team. The Cup was withheld and officially the results were expunged from the records. So this first match was not the Ryder Cup proper.

The first proper Ryder Cup match took place in Worcester Country Club, Massachusetts. Remarkably, the same British team was trounced by the Americans, establishing a familiar pattern. Ryder attended all the early matches in Britain. His great fear of sea travel prevented him from accompanying the team for the first official match in Worcester. He was ill when the British team set sail for the United States in 1935 and died early the following year.

In April 1929, the British team defeated the heavily-favoured Americans at Moortown Golf Club, Leeds. Anything less than a win might have brought the Ryder Cup concept to an early end. Lack of competition and apathy would have seen to that.

For its first twenty years the Ryder Cup matches were restricted to professionals from America and Britain. There was no Irish presence on the team until twenty years after its inception. Fred Daly (1911-90) was the first representative from this island to play in the Ryder Cup. It is clear that Daly was first and foremost a Loyalist Ulsterman and his allegiance to the Republic of Ireland was tenuous. This did not, however, deter him from playing as a Great Britain and Ireland player.

Fred Daly made his Ryder Cup début in 1947, an inauspicious start in a team that was beaten 11 to 1. In 1949 Daly recorded his first Ryder Cup points in Ganton GC, Scarborough, in a foursomes victory. Two years later in Pinehurst, Daly, playing against Clayton Heafner, rallied from three holes down with three to play, won them all and recorded half a point. It was one of the few bright moments in an otherwise predictable seven-point win for the Americans.

The typical British professional of the 1940s and 1950s was a club pro spending most of his time at his job, dependable if poorly-paid employment. Playing in international tournaments had to be fitted around the job, which made it very difficult to compete. Arthur Lees (1908-92), who was associated for nearly thirty years with Sunningdale golf club near London, managed to compete around Europe. He won the Irish Open in 1939 and competed in Germany and Czechoslovakia before the war. He won the 1947 Dunlop Masters and was twice winner of the Penfold event, in 1951 and 1953.

Competing in the Ryder Cup meant getting permission to take at least two weeks off from the club job. Crossing the Atlantic took five days. Add in the practice, the matches and the journey home. And then go directly back to work.

The Ryder Cup would certainly not have survived without the passion and commitment of professionals like Lees. He competed in four Cups (1947-51 and 1955) and was never on a winning team. In 1951 Lees gained the distinction of becoming the first British player to win both his foursomes and singles in the same Cup.

The Ryder Cup was held at Wentworth in 1953 and Harry Bradshaw joined Daly on the British and Irish team. Expectations were high; it was twenty years since the Americans had last been beaten. The American team featured six rookies and Ben Hogan decided not to compete. The British and Irish hopes were not unreasonable as this was an untried and shaky American team. The home team was put together under a new selection process – seventeen players were invited to Wentworth for trial matches watched by a tournament committee.

For the British and Irish this was perhaps the beginning of the modern approach to Ryder Cup preparation. The team stayed in the same hotel as the visitors, and captain Henry Cotton insisted that they practise together and hold nightly team meetings.

Cotton shrewdly paired Daly and Bradshaw, the first all-Irish pairing. They won by a hole against Cary Middlecoff and Walter Burkemo in a match that saw the Americans twice recover from 3-down. On the 34th hole the Americans could have squared the match. Bradshaw's drive was heading for the out of bounds when it hit a spectator and luckily landed back in play. Daly holed a tricky putt on the 18th for victory. Surprisingly, the Americans were up 3-1 at the end of the foursomes.

The home team launched the anticipated comeback in the singles matches and the teams were 4-4 after Harry Weetman defeated Sam Snead 1-up, Snead's only singles loss in seven appearances. Both Daly and Bradshaw won their singles matches comfortably but it wasn't enough to prevent the Americans from winning by one point. This was a competitive Cup and it rekindled the belief that the corner had been turned. For the first time, the word 'pressure' was used in relation to the matches.

The tournament returned to the US in 1955, a significant year for the Irish contingent. Christy O'Connor made his début, joining his friend Harry Bradshaw.

The British PGA changed the method of selecting players, a key development that should have been utilised many years before.

An Order of Merit was established based on the result of select tournaments. The top seven players would automatically qualify, leaving the committee to decide on the final three. This was a flawed selection process guided by the belief that it would produce 'in form' players. The American system of giving points for performance over two years was more effective: consistency was the key. O'Connor was one of four new faces on the Great Britain and Ireland team.

For the first time, players could choose between the larger American ball and the smaller British ball and were allowed to switch balls from hole to hole. The smaller ball was favoured on longer holes for greater distance and the larger ball was relied upon when control around the greens was important. This option prevailed until 1969.

Palm Springs, California, had the whiff of Hollywood about it in 1955 with the presence of Johnny Weismuller and parties at Frank Sinatra's house. The Americans prevailed 8-4 but the scoreline is deceiving. The singles matches produced plenty of drama with O'Connor falling 3 behind Tommy Bolt after 18 holes, only to regain the initiative amidst the predictable temper tantrums displayed by the American. Bolt overcame the Irishman 4-2 but it was not an easy victory.

Bradshaw versus Jack Burke was one of two remaining matches out on the course and a draw was still on the cards. In the morning Bradshaw shot a 65 to stay level with Burke. However, he was not able to maintain that level of performance in the afternoon. Burke took a three-hole lead at the turn and prevailed 3 and 2. It was a case of what might have been for Great Britain and Ireland. Four points was their best performance in America. Guarded optimism replaced the hopelessness and resignation to defeat of recent years.

The Great Britain and Ireland victory at Lindrick GC in 1957 was the first in twenty-four years and the excitement and celebrations were savoured. The match was memorable for bickering, nastiness and unsporting conduct. Bolt could not be appeased. Finsterwald's behaviour in his match with O'Connor was in poor taste.

David Feherty on O'Connor:

> Senior was, of course, a world-class player, capable of beating any opponent. Because of the times that were in it, the Americans never got to see O'Connor in his prime. The man could have won multiple Majors if circumstances were more favourable for travel. The man is a legend and rightly so.

The Great Britain and Ireland team was unable to build on the 1957 victory and order was restored two years later at Eldorado CC, Palm Desert, California. It was a tame, predicable affair with the Americans winning by five points. Norman Drew joined Christy O'Connor on the team, maintaining double representation from Ireland. Norman Drew of Bangor GC was the first Irish golfer to have represented Great Britain and Ireland at both Walker Cup and Ryder Cup level. He was synonymous with Bangor GC, as was the legendary amateur, Garth McGimpsey, in more recent times.

Drew distinguished himself in the singles matches, coming back from a four-hole deficit after nine holes against Doug Ford. At one point it looked as ifs Ford would close this match out early but Drew played gritty tenacious golf and reached the 18th hole with the American 1-up. Drew hit a wonderful 3-wood to the middle of the green and won the hold to earn a draw.

The Ryder Cup approached the 1960s. Only four Irish golfers had made the team since the matches began in 1927.

The ease of the 1959 victory brought into focus the one-sided nature of the Cup. In the five matches of the 1950s, the Americans had gone 4-1 and outscored their opponents 37-23. With a healthy supply of world-class talent emerging in the States in the 1960s, the prospects for improvement in the Great Britain and Ireland performances seemed as remote as ever.

There was a suggestion that the rest of Europe should be allowed to join the British, or failing that, the British should be allowed to recruit from the Commonwealth. That would have opened the way for Gary Player and Bobby Locke (South Africa) and the great Australian Peter Thomson, who would have considerably bolstered the team. Sadly, this idea was never seriously considered.

The 1961 matches at Royal Lytham and St Annes saw another US triumph – by five points. Notwithstanding the inevitable outcome, significant changes were made to the format, the first since 1927. All matches were shortened from thirty-six holes to eighteen. This would make the matches more marketable and television-friendly for the Americans and ease the burden of the thirty-six-hole marathon for the British.

A decision was made upon to play twice as many matches each day, doubling the number of total points from twelve to twenty-four. This change would reduce the likelihood of players qualifying and not playing. A suggestion that the event be extended from two days to three with the addition of fourball matches was not implemented.

The changes put more pressure on the captains as they needed to know how their players were doing in the morning to make substitutions in the afternoon. It was also the last time that both captains would play.

Great Britain and Ireland were routed 23-9 in 1963. A third day of play was added, as well as two rounds of fourballs. For the first time the British players travelled by plane, accompanied by their wives.

When the matches were played at Royal Birkdale in 1965 there was a noticeable improvement in amenities for spectators – tented village, mobile post office, food counters, lavatories and first aid. The golf writers now had their own building near the final green. The Americans were long used to hosting and organising big events and the lesson was not lost on the British.

Jimmy Martin joined O'Connor to make up the Irish contingent. The Americans were comfortable winners by 7 points.

Another whitewash in Texas in 1967 saw the usual clamour for changes that had been articulated over the years. The fifteen-point margin of victory suggested that a Great Britain and Ireland team was never likely to win the Cup.

At Royal Birkdale in 1969, the size of the squads was enlarged to twelve. Another change was the mandatory use of the larger American ball. Jack Nicklaus made his début for the Americans and conceded a putt to Tony Jacklin that would go into golfing folklore. The final score – 16 to 16 – was greeted with satisfaction by almost everybody.

Nicklaus was severely criticised by American captain Sam Snead for conceding the putt to Jacklin:

> When it happened, all the boys thought it was ridiculous to give him that putt. We went over there to win, not to be good ol' boys. I never would have given a putt like that – except maybe to my brother.

Nicklaus's gesture defused what had been a difficult week for the Ryder Cup, with a lot of bickering animosity.

Christy O'Connor made his last Ryder Cup appearance at Muirfield in 1973, aged forty-nine. It was a fitting conclusion to Senior's ten-year thirty-six-match Ryder Cup career. He battled Tom Weiskopf, then in his prime, all the way to the last green, where he got up and down from the sand to halve the hole and the match.

2

The Format of the Ryder Cup

Every two years, twelve men from the United States and twelve men from Europe compete for what is generally regarded as the pinnacle of professional golf – the Ryder Cup. Serious golf fans need no introduction to the format of the tournament.

Most golf tournaments around the world are decided by medal or stroke-play, over the course of a seventy-two-hole four-round tournament. The lowest score wins. The matchplay involved in the Ryder Cup is different in almost every respect. Each hole is won or lost or tied (which is called a half).

The match ends when one team is up by a number exceeding the number of holes left to play. For example, if one individual or team is 2-up with one hole to play, it is considered a 2 and 1 victory. There are twenty-eight matches in the Ryder Cup format. The first team to reach 14½ wins. If there is a 14-14 tie, the team that holds the Cup retains it.

Sixteen two-man team matches are played on Friday and Saturday, four in the morning, four in the afternoon. The morning competition is the alternate-shot, or foursomes. The players on each team alternate shots until the ball is holed, or the hole is conceded. This is where the role of the captain and his assistant becomes relevant. The caption must put together two players who are compatible and, based on the configuration of holes, have his best iron players hit into the par-threes, or his best driver teeing off at the tough par-fours.

The afternoon competition is the best ball or fourballs, again, two players from each team, each player playing his own ball. This format encourages more aggressive play and fans will invariably see a lot of birdies. The strategy here is to find the combination of players who can impose themselves and make things happen.

On Saturday night, each captain fills out a line-up card for the Sunday singles competition. There are twelve matches on Sunday unless there is an injury. Should this happen (as it did it 1991 and 1993), a designated player from the opposing team is 'put in the envelope' and must sit out. Each team then gets a half-point.

Not every putt needs to be holed out. Players can give putts or concede holes. This can lead to controversy – as in 1969, when Sam Snead was furious with Jack Nicklaus for conceding a putt to Tony Jacklin to halve their match – because it's a matter of interpretation as to what a 'gimme' putt is. In the 2006 Ryder Cup, Paul McGinley conceded a hole to after the intrusion of a streaker had unsettled both players and team captain Ian Woosnam was denied a record victory margin. Matchplay can bring out the best and worst in players. There is a pronounced element of psychology in action as the tension mounts in close contests.

While conceding a putt or hole may infuriate captains and team-mates, having an opponent putt out every time can cause animosity. Seve Ballasteros rarely gave a putt and was unrivalled when it came to the gamesmanship of matchplay. Ultimately, the magnanimous gestures are what endure in the folklore of the game. Nicklaus's concession is still talked about and was a milestone in the history of the game. It captured the essence of the Ryder Cup.

THE EARLY DAYS OF THE IRISH AND THE RYDER CUP
Any assessment of the Irish and the Ryder Cup has to acknowledge the tradition established by O'Connor, Harry Bradshaw, Fred Daly and several others, in an era when Great Britain and Ireland were routinely defeated, sometimes heavily. Fred Daly won the British Open in 1947 and should perhaps have added to his tally. Harry Bradshaw was unlucky not to win an Open. Sixty years would pass before the Claret Jug crossed the Irish Sea, thanks to Padraig Harrington's victory in 2007 (and again in 2008).

O'Connor never won a British Open but his greatness owed much to his many gallant battles to win what was then the only Major for European players. He finished one shot behind Peter Thomson at Royal Lytham and St Annes in 1958, an Open that most observers believed he should have won.

On the final hole, O'Connor needed a birdie-3 to win or a par-4 for a tie and playoff. He had earlier become frustrated with Thomson's slow pace of play and filed a complaint about this gamesmanship. Thomson was already in the clubhouse as O'Connor readied to tee off, or so he thought. The enthusiastic crowds were beyond the capabilities of the stewards but after ten minutes order of a kind was restored, even though the crowds had obscured the right-hand side of the fairway.

O'Connor hit a 3-wood instead of his driver to avoid the bunkers on the left, now that the fairway was narrowed. The crowd reaction indicated a good shot but when he found his ball it was embedded in the sand 160 yards from the green. He had no option but to play for safety and hope to get up and down with his third shot. What would have been a routine par (at least) was not to be.

O'Connor was second to Thomson at Royal Birkdale in 1965. His degree of excellence at the Open is revealed by the following figures. Between 1955 and 1974, he made ten top-ten finishes and he was in the top twenty on fourteen other occasions. O'Connor became an iconic figure when the Carroll's Irish Open was broadcast on Irish television. His victories caught the imagination of the Irish public and his Arnold Palmer-like charges became a feature of those tournaments.

A Major eluded him; going to the Masters was not financially feasible and April came too soon for O'Connor after a lack of quality practice in the Irish winters. He recorded fifty tournament victories at home and abroad and represented Ireland in the World Cup of Golf on fifteen occasions.

He achieved a memorable victory with Harry Bradshaw in Mexico City in 1958. O'Connor also made ten appearances in the Ryder Cup, the highlight of which was a victory for Great Britain and Ireland in an incident-packed 1957 match at Lindrick. He played against the American, Dow Finsterwald, trouncing him 7 and 6 in the final day's singles. It was a match characterised by recrimination and argument. Finsterwald would not shake hands with O'Connor when the match finished and declined to do so later when exhorted to do so by his own team-mates.

O'Connor was a world-class player and played his best golf against the world's best. Winning a Major title would have been the pinnacle for this legend; nonetheless, the lack of a Major does not diminish his greatness in any way. Like Bradshaw and Joe Carr, Christy was an ambassador for Ireland and his reputation preceded him wherever he played. He set and maintained the highest standards and became a touchstone for succeeding generations of top-class Irish players.

Peter Alliss expresses this better than most in his assessment:

Long before we had the present glut of team competitions, i.e the Seve Trophy, President's Cup, the PGA matches and the Solheim Cup, there was the Ryder Cup, which started its life in the mid-1920s. My father, Percy, played a number of times but because he was domiciled abroad, as indeed were Henry Cotton and Aubrey Boomer (possibly the three best players in British golf at that time), the number of appearances he made was limited.

My chance came in 1953 but it wasn't until 1957 that I met Christy O'Connor. He made his début in Ryder Cup play in 1955 and, although he didn't play in the foursomes, he led the way in the singles but was beaten 4 and 2 by Tommy Bolt. I first met up with Christy in the matchplay at Lindrick Golf Club in 1957, where he lost his foursomes, playing alongside another great character, Eric Brown, to Dick Mayer and, again, Tommy Bolt, but in the singles he was victorious to the tune of 7 and 6 over the very fine professional player, Dow Finsterwald.

We first played together in the matches at Palm Springs in 1959, where we beat Doug Ford and Art Wall 4 and 2 in the foursomes. We were again partnered in 1961 at Royal Lytham and St Annes, where we led the home team in the foursomes and beat Doug Ford and Gene Littler 4 and 3. It was a different story in the afternoon when we were beaten by one hole by Art Wall and Jay Hebert.

For some reason, when the matches were played in Atlanta, Georgia, in 1963, after a losing opening match our partnership was broken up. By this time it was decided we would have 18-hole matches and play morning and afternoon, rather than the 36-hole affairs that had been the case since the Ryder Cup's inception. The matches in 1965 produced probably our finest hour; we won three and lost only one of the four matches we were involved in. The last time we played together in the Ryder Cup was in 1969, where we managed to halve our foursomes against Billy Casper and Frank Beard; and that was the end of it.

We'd had a wonderful run and I couldn't have wished for a finer partner. He was one of the purest strikers of the golf ball it's ever been my privilege to play with or watch. The only thing that was erratic was his putting; when he was on form he was irresistible but there were moments of frailty.

We had a wonderful rapport and Christy's professionalism on the golf course was second to none. It was a pleasure to partner him and although it was a difficult time for British and Irish golf, as we were pretty well outgunned by the might of America, we had great success and our losses, when you consider that many were played over 36 holes, were very tight affairs.

In October 2007 the Lindrick Golf Club held a

fiftieth-anniversary celebration of that great victory. There are only three members of that original team left – Bernard Hunt, Christy O'Connor and myself. Christy, sadly, wasn't quite up to the journey although he's in pretty good health but he was there in spirit and sadly missed. One of Ireland's greatest!

In the 1967 Ryder Cup, the United States crushed the British and Irish 23½ to 8½ in Houston, Texas. The defeat was not unexpected but the margin of victory was the source of considerable concern. 'It's dying fast,' proclaimed the editorial of *Irish Golf* in its December issue. 'Times and attitudes are changing but even now, there are golf clubs where a man who's won every honour in the paid game would not be allowed in the members' bar. And of course, there is that British attitude – shared by some foolish people in this country – that to try to win at all costs, like the Americans, is not in very good taste.'

The times did indeed change and the taste of success laid the foundation for a winning attitude in Europe. The bleak outlook of *Irish Golf* at the end of 1967 was anything but prescient – the British and Irish tied the Americans in the 1969 matches at Royal Birkdale.

The breakthrough was finally achieved at the Belfry in 1985 – albeit under an expanded European team – and writ large two years later. It is no small irony that Jack Nicklaus's vision for a European team should come back to haunt him and inflict upon the Americans their first ever home defeat at Muirfield Village, designed by Nicklaus, under the captaincy of the 'Golden Bear' himself. It was surely a bittersweet moment for the American legend but it was entirely appropriate that it happened during the tenure of a captain as magnanimous as him.

A little over a decade later the Ryder Cup was on its way to becoming the most popular event in golf. The competition brought in an estimated $150 million at Brookline in 1999.

3

EAMONN DARCY, ASTRIDE TWO ERAS: A TRIUMPH OF ENDURANCE

We were in America in 1987, at Jack's Muirfield Village in Ohio. Jack was captain of the American team, the first American team in a generation trying to earn the Ryder Cup back. By this time I was well seasoned in the captain's role and I fully understood that it was my job to give the players everything I could to make them as comfortable as possible, to do whatever I could to take the pressure off them in every way, shape and form.

I wanted them to be thinking about one thing and one thing only: performing to the limit of their abilities. It was about me doing my best so that they could do their best. My job was to not piss anyone off, because if they were pissed off, they weren't going to perform to that outer limit.

Tony Jacklin

Eamonn Darcy turned professional in 1971. The records show that over the ensuing thirty years he won four titles – the 1977 Greater Manchester Open, the 1983 Benson and Hedges Spanish Open, the 1987 Volvo Belgian Open and the 1990 Emirates Airlines Desert Classic. At first glance this is a meagre return but it doesn't begin to measure the achievements of a lifetime on the European Tour.

There are intangibles that cannot be quantified, for example a tie for fourth place in the Murphy's Irish Open at Druid's Glen in 1999, twenty-eight years after Darcy had turned pro. This was a satisfying accomplishment for him as he was the club professional at Druid's Glen. He was the leading Irishman in the Irish Open that year.

'I really felt the pressure, being the home club pro,' he recalled. 'The crowds and atmosphere were great.'

At the age of forty-eight he shot a 64, a new course record, in the second round of the 2001 Smurfit Irish PGA Championship at Baltray. The previous record, 65,was posted by Jimmy Hegarty in 1985.

He had competed in over 700 events when he retired from the Tour in 2002 at the age of forty-nine. His career winnings amounted to over £2 million, another anomaly given that for much of his early career there was very little to be made as a professional golfer. , Darcy has no regrets:

> There have been a lot of highlights in my career, priceless memories, events, people, experiences. You can't put a money value on that. The Ryder Cup is one of the biggest.

Darcy made his Ryder Cup début in 1975 with two other Irishmen, Christy O'Connor Jr and John O'Leary. In all, that Great Britain and Ireland team contained six rookies. The result was a foregone conclusion and it turned out to be another damage-limitation exercise for the visiting team. The American team was captained by Arnold Palmer and the matches were held at Laurel Valley, a club Palmer had been associated with for years as a 'playing professional', because of its proximity to his hometown of Latrobe, Pennsylvania.

It rained heavily in the days leading up to the contest. Practice rounds were cancelled. Palmer's allure was strong enough to attract 10,000 fans each day. It turned into a rout by the Americans from the first day and as the Sunday singles approached the Americans had a hefty lead, needing only 3½ points from the sixteen singles matches to win. The only memorable contest was between Jack Nicklaus and Brian Barnes. The big Englishman beat Nicklaus in the last of the morning singles. Palmer contrived that the two players would meet in the afternoon, only for Barnes to beat Nicklaus a second time.

'The American team was a cannon,' says Feherty, 'and Great Britain sent over a pop-gun.' Darcy and Guy Hunt managed to gain a half-point in the foursomes against Al Geiberger and Raymond Floyd. In the singles, Bill Casper defeated Darcy by 3 and 2. According to the press the Ryder Cup was dying if not already dead. *Golf World* magazine chimed in with a cruel observation: 'The British are a team that has not proved it could master even the American Walker Cup team.'

Darcy was the only Irish representative in the Great Britain and Ireland team that faced the Americans at Royal Lytham and St Annes in 1977. There was a change in format but the result was another comprehensive victory for the Americans. In the opening foursomes, Darcy and Jacklin managed a half against Sam Sneed and Don January.

Brian Hugget was not one of the most effective captains ever to lead a Great Britain and Ireland team. The 1977 Cup will be remembered for his treatment of Tony Jacklin, who was dropped from the singles matches.

Darcy fought a dogged match with Hubert Green before losing at the 18th hole. 'Green and Darcy staged a good fight,' Feherty says, 'although their two swings made several people in the crowd faint.' Darcy's reputation as a Ryder Cup player was enhanced even in defeat. The next time Darcy played Ryder Cup it would be for a European team. The 1977 contest brought an end to the Great Britain and Ireland selection.

Darcy's next appearance in the Ryder Cup came in 1981, at Walton Heath GC in Surrey. The Europeans were soundly beaten by the Americans, who had a substantial nine-point margin. Before Darcy and Nicklaus teed off in the final match of the day, the Cup was in American hands. Lee Trevino was back in the clubhouse, having defeated Sam Torrance 5 and 3. This would be his last Ryder Cup appearance.

He joked that he would gladly play again if Nicklaus wanted to stay out of the rain. Trevino went 4-0 at Walton Heath. Nicklaus easily accounted for Darcy 5 and 3. The heavy rains and wind that dogged the tournament all week added to the gloom.

The European Ryder Cup teams of 1983 and 1985 featured no Irish players. Darcy qualified for the 1987 team that went to America to defend the trophy. For Darcy, the lone Irishman on the team, this would be his defining Ryder Cup.

THE 1987 RYDER CUP, MUIRFIELD VILLAGE, DUBLIN, OHIO

It's hard to pinpoint a moment when golf got cool. Formerly the province of the rich, fat white guys, in the mid-1980s it became the obsession of movie stars and CEOs, pop stars and politicians. Baby boomers whose knees hurt from tennis and jogging fell in love with a game that let them spend wads of money on equipment, was perfect for business and entertaining and demanded little or no physical exertion: for many, the real fun was racing around in electric carts with multiple cup holders.

During this explosion, the Ryder Cup benefited because it was unique – a team event played for national pride. The excitement came to a head at the 1987 matches, which for the first time since 1959 were being held on US soil with the Cup not gathering dust in an American closet.

David Feherty

Because of a selection system based on the points players had won over the previous two years, and the current US Open and PGA champions earning automatic berths, this 1987 US team was one of the weakest ever, featuring five rookies. The Europeans had a team that was experienced and playing well.

Europe team captain Tony Jacklin remembers:

I was blessed with an incredible roster of upper echelon talent. Nothing against fellows like Howard Clark or Eamonn Darcy; they were great players, fighters and they worked like hell for that team. Eamonn, in particular, was magnificent in beating Crenshaw in the singles. But I just felt that year we were going to live or die by the performance of our big guns, so I decided to ride them hard.

The Americans trailed 6-2 at the end of the first day and won the second day's matches 4½-3½. Heading into the singles, Europe needed 3½ points and the Americans an unlikely 9. To their credit they made an impressive run and came close to pulling off a spectacular upset. With a little over half the matches finished, the Americans had closed the deficit to one point. The Darcy-Crenshaw match now took on an added significance. Weak team or not, the Americans were quite capable of salvaging what seemed a hopeless cause. Eight of the matches went to the last hole and the outcome was in the balance.

After 3-putting the 6th hole to go 2 down, Crenshaw, in an uncharacteristic fit of temper, snapped his putter, breaking the shaft and making it ineligible for further use. Gentle Ben, renowned for his dignified bearing and reverence for the history of the game, was anything but dignified on this day.

'He lost the rag for sure,' Feherty says,

> Who would have envisaged that? He not only broke his beloved Wilson 8802 putter, he beat the living shit out of it. This sweet-natured soul had turned into a raging bull but the bastard never lost his composure.

Putting with his one-iron and sand wedge he got himself back into the match and took the lead with a birdie at the par-3 16th. He lost the lead at the 17th by flying the green and missing it in 3. They headed to 18 with a vital point at stake.

Watching the two players address their ball and swing, one could be forgiven for wondering how Darcy stayed in this match. Crenshaw, a proud Texan, was noted for his classic free-flowing swing, textbook stuff. Darcy had a distinctive swing with too many moving parts, a loop in the backswing and a limited follow-through. A thing of beauty it was not. J.B. Carr would have called it an agricultural swing, similar to his own. Like many others, it was the swing that best suited Darcy and invariably, the club met the ball and got it in play effectively. As Carr used to say, 'Hitters linger, swingers last.'

Both Crenshaw and Darcy were accomplished putters with a sure putting touch. Putting on the lightning-fast green at Muirfield would decide the outcome of this match. Crenshaw's classic swing faltered on 18, where he hit his second crooked tee shot in a row. He hooked his initial drive left into the water. He took a penalty drop and with his third shot managed to advance the ball into a greenside bunker. Darcy's ball was in the same bunker but he had a stroke advantage.

Crenshaw played first, a fine shot that ran further than he expected. The tension was matched only by the respectful silence as thousands waited around the green with millions more in America and Europe watching the match on television. Darcy splashed his shot to within five feet of the hole.

Using his 3-iron, Crenshaw masterfully rolled the ball into the hole for a bogey 5.

Darcy was left with a five-foot putt for the win. This was a tricky, nervy shot – a downhill putt with a deceptive left-to-right swing. No one truly knows how Darcy felt as he stood over that putt. He was certainly aware of its significance. His putting touch didn't desert him in this most crucial moment and he rolled it smoothly into the hole for the win and a vital point for the Europeans. Darcy's win meant that Europe needed just 1½ points from the final five games.

Ballasteros may have struck the winning putt in closing out Curtis Strange on the 17th hole but Darcy was the unlikely hero. This was Darcy's first win in eleven matches over four years. 'It was a timely win made even better because it effectively killed off the

American challenge,' Darcy said. Jack Nicklaus, gracious in defeat, acknowledged Darcy's contribution: 'I would put Darcy's putt as the final nail in our coffin. He holed it like a man and the memory should live with him forever!'

This was a generous and magnanimous tribute, typical of the qualities that endeared Nicklaus to golf fans the world over. He also made the pertinent observation that his players didn't win the 18th hole in any match. The remark hinted at complacency among the American players, who made considerable money by playing percentage golf. This blunted the aggressive approach necessary to win the Ryder Cup, an aggression the Europeans had in abundance as there were so many players competing for much less money.

This was undoubtedly one of the highlights of Darcy's long career. Sam Torrance felt that Darcy was never the same again after that match. Although well-intentioned, the Scot got it wrong in this instance. Unlike Ronan Rafferty and Philip Walton, Darcy kept his game and his card for several years after his Ryder Cup experience, no small achievement.

NO REGRETS

> At the end of the day we play for cash but when it is a team event it is much sweeter; when you play you're representing your country. That's why the Dunhill Cup win [Darcy captained Ireland to Dunhill victory with Ronan Rafferty and Des Smyth in 1988] was so memorable. The Ryder Cup is one of the biggest highlights and the obvious one. When I captained Ireland in the Dunhill Cup that was a great win for Ireland.
>
> Eamonn Darcy

Like many of the players from his era, Darcy feels that the younger players are not getting the same enjoyment from the game:

We had great fun and it all seemed so easy then. We had a few jars and still shot 68. We didn't beat ourselves up over the socialising. When you're young you just go out, you don't give a hoot, just go and play.

I think many of the players are far too serious now. The stakes are higher and there is so much more money and media attention. There should be a happy medium, though; otherwise a youngster might not stay with it. I'm not saying they should be out drinking, far from it.

We played because we loved the game, we were passionate about it and I'd be happy to play for a few quid with the lads.

I'm not envious in the least. There is so much more available to the players now and good luck to them. I have no regrets about my career. I got a great lash out of it and the memories I have could not be bought.

4

Des Smyth: a Lifelong Love of the Game

Des Smyth recalls a remarkable encounter with his hero, Jack Nicklaus, on his way out of the car park at the 2003 British Seniors Open:

> I know Jack but not real well. I saw him walking down the car park. About ninety minutes earlier he was flying on the golf course. He had a bit of a setback the last four holes. Anyway, I rolled the window down and asked him how he finished, because it looked like he was going to shoot a 63, which is his age. He ended up with a 65 and went into this description of the last five holes in detail.
>
> He had his head stuck inside the car for about twenty-five minutes and he probably didn't even see me when he was giving me the details. He was so involved: this meant so much to him and he had failed. That's what struck me. That, I thought, was just fantastic. Here's the greatest player who ever played golf – his record proves it and Tiger has a long way to go – and he was in a trance of disappointment... because he didn't shoot a 63.
>
> That's what brought it home to me. It means so much to these guys. It wasn't the money, it wasn't the glory. It was that he thought he could do it and he was gutted. His last words to me were: 'Well, I'll try again tomorrow.' The great ones love the game and they love to play the best that they can possibly play.

What Smyth recognised in Nicklaus was his own love and passion for the game: working on something new, a different shot, a perceived weakness. Smyth was the obvious choice for captain of the European team when the Ryder Cup was played at the K Club in 2006. That he was made a vice-captain was inadequate. Ian Woosnam was a brilliant captain but the Irish contribution to the Ryder Cup merited an Irish captain. Smyth accepted his vice-captain's role with dignity and equanimity but a golden opportunity to acknowledge the historic Irish association with the competition was lost. Smythy understands how these things are decided and the politicking involved. Similarly, Bernhard Langer, captain in 2004, lamented the fact that the Ryder Cup would not be played on German soil until at least 2016.

Des Smyth is an easygoing, unassuming and modest man, hugely popular with fellow-golfers and fans alike. He doesn't show a trace of bitterness when it comes to the question of inadequate accolades. For Smyth, the game is all that matters: the last round, the next shot, the excitement and passion that these inspire.

Des Smyth's golf career may not have scaled the heights. He didn't make a Ryder Cup winning shot, he won no Majors. What defines Smyth's career in professional golf is its longevity. When he started out as a pro in the European Tour it was unlike the modern Tour in so many ways – small money, wearisome travelling, unremarkable accommodation and none of the perks and cosseting that are the norm in the modern game. It was a precarious lifestyle, without the big sponsorships, equipment deals or television. Financially, there was little change since Christy O'Connor Sr won the biggest cheque in history back in the 1960s.

THE SWINGING SEVENTIES

Des Smyth played his early golf as a schoolboy for St Joseph's CBS, Drogheda, and went on to compete for the school in the Irish Schools' Championships. One of his early opponents was Arthur Pierse of Tipperary, who played for Rockwell College. Pierse went on to be one of the country's leading amateurs and played for Munster, Ireland and Great Britain and Ireland. He might have turned professional like Smyth but the family business came first.

In the summer of 1977, Pierse and Smyth took the ferry together from Larne to Stranraer in Scotland. They had become friendly over the course of various competitions, so they headed for Scotland and pooled their resources to save money. Their ambition was to pre-qualify for the British Open, to be held the following week at Turnberry. Pierse's twin brother Gerry was roped in as caddie.

Both young men achieved qualification in the starting line-up in what became known as 'the duel in the sun' between Jack Nicklaus and Tom Watson. They played only a bit part but to them it was more adventure than competition, watching their heroes. Pierse remembers that at one stage in the build-up to the Open, the Irish pair shared the practice ground with Nicklaus, Watson and Trevino:

> It ended up with Dessie getting a lesson from Watson. We had a long conversation with him. He was telling us how important it was to build up our arms and our legs, that strong arms and legs were needed for golf. That was 1977, so all the talk about Tiger being the lad who brought everybody into weights is absolutely untrue. All these guys did it and Gary Player was the first, of course.

Twenty-five years on, Smyth would cross paths with Watson again when making a highly successful foray into the Champions Tour in America. Pierse, however, explains why he eschewed the professional ranks:

> In the 1970s, professional golf wasn't like it is today. Very few top amateurs, except for John O'Leary and Des, turned pro because the money wasn't in it. The Open was always live on television but the money only really started to grow in golf after 1980, when television began to do more outside broadcasts and that brought increased interest in the game. I considered turning pro but could I make a livelihood from playing golf? I decided that I

couldn't and that I probably had a better chance of being successful by going into a business.

Christy O'Connor Sr was an early inspiration and significant influence on Smyth and on so many other golfers, both professional and amateur. O'Connor was a world-class striker of the ball, perhaps unrivalled in his prime. What was noteworthy about O'Connor was the durability of his swing, which commanded attention well after he was fifty. Smyth was in awe of what the older pro could do. 'If you were fortunate enough to see him play,' Smyth says:

> You just stood back and watched him swing. He looked so entirely natural swinging a golf club. It was a privilege to watch him and play with him.
>
> When you were a kid you heard of him…then you got sight of him…and then you were lucky to play with him. He was a player ahead of his time in his technical ability. There was a purity about the way he hit the ball. His chipping was marvellous and if he saw a shot he went after it, regardless of how difficult it might be.
>
> As a player he was tough, single-minded. You'd notice the concentration and the way he went about playing his golf. He managed to make it look so natural. You had to be influenced by this. It was something you wanted to emulate. And he always had an encouraging word for up-and-coming players and he was accessible to them with his knowledge and experience. So yes, like many others I have to credit Christy's influence.
>
> You couldn't find a better player as a role model.

Smyth turned pro in 1974.

> People often ask me why I turned pro. It wasn't for the money because there wasn't any in golf. Even the top pros didn't make huge dough. I had a love affair

with the game. I played kids' golf at Laytown and Bettystown. I won my first trophy when I was seven.

I played Barton Cup, represented Leinster at junior and senior level, then progressed to international level. That's how I got into the game and I have been involved in it ever since.

It was this passion that enabled Smyth to cope with the vagaries of the game, especially in the early years when things weren't so good.

I always had motivation and a disappointment never put me off. It was never the end of the world for me. As I came through as a young player I played lots of great golf but I played lots of bad golf too and I always considered that part of the package. Nowadays when I see guys playing badly you'd think it was the end of the world. I laugh when I see it because it's only a phase.

The modern player relies a lot more on psychologists, physiotherapists, dieticians and so on. Maybe it's a reflection of the times we live in. My generation generally had less and were more self-reliant: you wouldn't be caught dead talking to a psychologist.

But if it works for players – and many seem very dependent on them – then by all means avail of them. When psychologists were introduced to the Tour I tried one or two of them just to see what it was about but it really wasn't for me. The same goes for much of the incredible technology available today.

I'm not much of a gadget guy. I'd rather read the newspapers than look at a computer. I'm probably an exception. Neither would I be too fixated on statistics, although it's hard to avoid them nowadays. Statistics never hit a drive or stood over a putt. I just play the best I can.

RYDER CUP 1979: THE GREENBRIER, WHITE SULPHUR SPRINGS, WEST VIRGINIA

In 1979, for the first time, Continental Europe was added to Great Britain and Ireland, broadening the pool for team selection. There would be no immediate success but the significant change had been effected. In 1971, the British PGA launched the European Tour and the top ten from their Tour's money-list would gain automatic selection, plus two captain's picks. John Jacobs was captain, a former Ryder Cup player better known as a golf instructor and golf administrator.

The First European team

Seve Ballasteros
Brian Barnes
Ken Brown
Nick Faldo
Bernard Gallacher
Antonio Garrido
Tony Jacklin
Mark James
Michael King
Sandy Lyle
Peter Oosterhuis*
Des Smyth*

(*Captain's picks)

Smyth's début in the Cup was inauspicious and was not helped by the behaviour of Ken Brown, his playing partner in the first day afternoon foursomes. They were soundly beaten 7 and 6 by Hale Irwin and Tom Kite. It was clear that Brown wasn't happy with Smyth and this was reflected in the way he played. He wanted to continue the partnership with his friend Mark James. He barely spoke a word to Smyth, a rookie. They recorded seven bogeys and two pars in the first nine holes. Their loss was the worst in Ryder Cup history up to that point.

Hale Irwin described what took place:

> Ken just hit some terrible shots. Des hit some good ones but when he did Ken promptly put him over in jail somewhere. I felt it was obvious there was no rapport between them. There was not even the slightest bit of idle conversation. Smyth didn't play very well and Brown played like he didn't care.

With the singles matches to go on Sunday, the Europeans, somewhat surprisingly, had clawed themselves back into contention and were behind by one point, 8½-7½.

After a bright start by the Europeans, the Americans won five matches and finished the singles 8-3. Four of those losses for the Europeans went to the final hole. Smyth lost to Irwin by 5 and 3. The matches were closer than the score suggests and the Europeans took a lot of positives from that experience. A bright future was certainly in store once Ballasteros, Faldo and Lyle began to win the Majors.

RYDER CUP 1981: WALTON HEATH GC, SURREY, ENGLAND

John Jacobs returned for his second stint as the European captain. As in 1979, the top ten players were to come directly from the European Order of Merit, with two picks made by a three-man committee that included the captain. Ballasteros, the 1980 Masters champion, should have been an automatic pick but fell foul of the European Tour.

Incredibly, he was voted out by Neil Coles and Bernhard Langer for not supporting the European Tour. According to Feherty:

> Seve's only supporter was Jacobs, who as team-captain was smart enough to put up with the trouble to get the talent. But Seve was out on his hole in every respect.

I would have picked the guy had be been playing in the outer Hebrides or Mars but those guys got it dead wrong.

Des Smyth had no such difficulties but the Europeans were up against a formidable American team – players that between them had won thirty-six Majors, including three that year. The European team, minus Ballasteros, had none.

Before the matches were played a heated controversy raged over the site selection. The Belfry got the nod but was subsequently rejected in favour of Walton Heath, a heathland course south of London. The Belfry, a few years old and the new headquarters of the British PGA, would inevitably get its turn, perhaps too many times.

The Europeans made a surprisingly good start, contrary to expectations, by halving the morning's foursomes. Des Smyth and Bernard Gallacher beat Hale Irwin and Raymond Floyd 3 and 2 as the rain came down.

In the afternoon fourballs, both captains shuffled their line-ups and despite rain interruptions, the Europeans continued to play well. Smyth was paired with Jose Maria Canizares, which raised a few eyebrows and attracted no little criticism. This supposedly weak pairing had no trouble defeating Bruce Lietzke and Bill Rogers by 6 and 5. The Europeans emerged with the lead at the end of the first day, 4½-3 ½.

On Saturday the resurgent Americans won the day 7-1. Smyth and Canizares were unfortunate to play a rested Tom Watson and Jack Nicklaus and were flattered by the 3 and 2 defeat. In the afternoon, Smyth and Gallacher went down 3 and 2 to Tom Kite and Larry Nelson.

The Europeans were 5 points down heading into the Sunday singles. The continued heavy downpour added to the gloom and they never got going against the Americans. Smyth went down to Crenshaw by 6 and 4. The Americans took the singles 8 to 4 for a comprehensive 9-point victory.

It was Smyth's last appearance in the Ryder Cup and although he didn't perform as well on the second and third days – the American team were unbeatable – he played with distinction on the first day and could be relatively satisfied with his contribution. He departed the scene before the Europeans blew the lid off the Ryder Cup, starting in 1983.

Smyth's Ryder Cup days were over but he continued to ply his trade on the European Tour. It was a remarkable feat for him to win the Madeira Open at the age of forty-eight, the Tour's oldest winner. This allowed him a further two-year exemption on the Tour, enabling him to achieve an unbroken thirty-year run.

He didn't made a great deal amount of money in that time but the intangibles he gained cannot be quantified. Indeed, when he began competing on the American Seniors (Champions Tour) the prize money involved was greater than any on offer when he was in his prime. Smyth gave himself a five-year window of opportunity on the Seniors Tour: 'That's my retirement fund,' he often joked.

Many of Smyth's finer moments came in the Dunhill Cup; he played in five Irish teams including the victorious team of 1988. This victory encapsulated all that was best in Smyth's golf career.

His caddie at the time was the legendary John O'Reilly. To say that O'Reilly is a character is an understatement. For twenty-five years he carried the bags of Peter Townsend, Des Smyth and Padraig Harrington. During that time he became one of the most colourful characters in the world of professional golf.

He linked up with Smyth for what would be a roller-coaster fifteen-year relationship. The Smyth-O'Reilly partnership played a crucial role in Ireland's victory in the Dunhill Cup in 1988. This is how O'Reilly remembered those glory days:

> I think the Dunhill Cup would be my favourite story. Ronan Rafferty, Eamonn Darcy and Smythy were playing for Ireland and had reached the semi-final stage to face England. Smythy was up against Nick Faldo, who was the main man in them days.

We got to the Tom Morris – which is what they call the last hole at St Andrews – and we were 1-up. The team was depending on a result. Faldo started complaining that he couldn't see properly but they both agreed to try and finish. Both of them hit good drives and then Smythy hit his second shot thirty feet over the green, leaving a long putt. Not ideal.

It was then that Nick decided that he wasn't playing on. He was well within his rights but he wasn't making any friends, I can tell you. At 6 am the next morning in the freezing cold, both of them were rehearsing the shots they were about to face. Half of Scotland seemed to have turned up and all the students from the university, who had windows overlooking the 18th green, had put up derogatory banners about Faldo. They weren't going to support an Englishman.

Well Smythy hit his putt to leave a nightmare four-footer, while Faldo's chip clipped the hole tantalisingly and stayed out. Des stood up to the pressure, though, and nailed his putt into the back of the hole. Before we knew it we were out for the final against the Australians. We won the whole tournament but it was the win against Faldo that I'll remember. Everybody expected him to turn Des over. Great satisfaction that was.

O'Reilly's days as a bagman for Smyth ended abruptly when he fell and broke two vertebrae in his back.

I was staying with Paul McGinley, Darren Clarke and Philip Walton in a basement apartment in Spain. It was Monday and the practice round had been abandoned because of torrential rain. We went out on the town and no better guys for letting their hair down and enjoying themselves than this lot.

When we got home, the steps, which were made of railroad ties, were wet and greasy. I was carrying one of Darren's cases when I slipped and fell, taking McGinley with me. I was totally paralysed, so Darren carried me to bed. Later in hospital in Malaga, I discovered I'd broken my wrist and broken my back.

I was off for nearly a year and had to walk with a harness on. But Darren and Paul looked after me, sending me cheques to tide me over. And not only them, all the guys in the PGA, from Ken Schofield down, were great. They got me on a private jet and got me home to hospital. They did everything possible and I really appreciated that.

Des Smyth is a level-headed and well-rounded family man. He has been able to maintain a consistently high level of competitive play, while, away from golf, his wife and children have prospered. He plans his golfing itinerary with his family's interest in mind and it is now rare for him to stay away for more than four weeks at a stretch:

I was very fortunate to pick golf because there can't be very many competitive sports which allow participants to play at the highest level for such a long period. It has never been difficult for me to be competitive. I've always enjoyed the challenge and it has been my ambition to keep my game up to the highest possible standard. Apart from the satisfaction of individual victories, it was just as gratifying to have held my place in the top twenty in Europe for such a long spell. From 1979 to 1989 I missed the top twenty only twice.

When you realise that there are fifty-five new players in the Tour each year, the pressure is on to make the top hundred and fifteen and I suppose it reflects the effort and the preparation that I've put in that I'm still out there. Basically, I'm a player's player and I'm constantly working on my game. But one also has to be realistic and one's targets must be realistic.

No one can expect to be a winner all the time and my best time was during the 1980s. In addition to winning a good few tournaments I played in my second Ryder Cup in 1981 and then there were the World Cups, the Hennessy Cognac Cup and the Dunhill Cup matches. It really was a great decade for me...my time really.

There's only a certain period when you can expect to be rated as a likely winner every time you start And I'm happy to accept the real situation. I was so fortunate to have been able to enjoy the European Tour for so long and I always wanted to finish on the Tour. That's why winning in Madeira was so satisfying. I avoided the pressure of having to qualify to maintain my card. It would have been very difficult after such a long time to have to search for invitations to play in tournaments one had been playing in automatically for twenty-five years.

In 2002, Smythy spoke of the possibility of being captain of the European Ryder Cup team:

The sheer honour would be fantastic. I've a strong feeling it will be an Irishman and, you know, it wouldn't be before its time. When you consider how much Ireland and Irish players have contributed to the Ryder Cup over the years, it's amazing that there has never been an Irish captain. From my point of view, I would love to be involved, particularly as I've been so close to the players on the tour for so long.

Smyth's comments reflected the popular sentiment in favour of an Irish captain. How appropriate it would have been for Smyth to emulate his hero Jack Nicklaus, who had captained the American team.

As the 2002 competition, approached the debate began to get contentious. Jose Maria Olazabal declared: 'It should come down to the individual merits of the respective captains, regardless of nationality. Ireland has produced a lot of good players but I don't think many of them were of the level that Seve [Ballesteros] was at.'

This was hardly a fair comment and Christy O'Connor Jr took issue with the Spaniard: 'Jose has his opinions but what other country has a finer input into the Ryder Cup than Ireland? Guys like Des and Eamonn have been there a lot longer than Jose.'

Smyth added:

> Irishmen have been on the Ryder Cup team from the beginning and there has never been an Irish captain. I find that extraordinary. I really feel that there should be an Irish captain for 2006. I won't be disappointed if it's not me but I will be hugely disappointed if it isn't an Irishman. And I think the Irish people will be hugely disappointed.

Disappointment was the order of the day for players and fans who hoped for an Irish captain in 2006. That Des Smyth became vice-captain was some compensation.

5

Christy Junior: in the Shadow of a Legend

> The definitive moment of the whole competition, in the
> end, was Christy O'Connor Jr beating Fred Couples.
> Freddie's a good fellow but I'm telling you I saw it all
> coming. Or at least I saw something coming.
>
> Tony Jacklin

The 1989 Ryder Cup, held in the Belfry Golf Club in the English
west midlands, was a definitive affirmation of Jacklin's success as
captain. He lead the Europeans to a third successive victory over the
Americans, an unprecedented achievement and a triumph for his
handling of players and player combinations.

Admittedly, he was leading a hugely talented group of European
players, who had won several Majors between them. Eight players
from the Muirfield Village team of 1987 were back. Two Irish
players qualified – the rookie Ronan Rafferty and Christy O'Connor
Jr, who hadn't played since 1975. On paper the Europeans were a
formidable team but Jacklin knew better than most that reputations
did not necessarily translate to success in Ryder Cup competition. It
was this awareness, combined with an element of good fortune, that
set him apart.

Raymond Floyd revealed his lack of tact as American captain
before the competition began. At the pre-match dinner, he introduced
his team as 'the twelve greatest players in the world', reminiscent of
the words of his predecessor Ben Hogan in 1967. Hogan had a case,
even if the comments were insensitive; Floyd was well wide of the
mark and even the American players were aware of that. His well-

intentioned comments would came back to haunt him.

The Americans opened with a 3-1 lead but the Europeans took all the afternoon fourballs and edged ahead 5-3, a lead they did not relinquish.

The Saturday matches ended 4-4 and with the support of a boisterous crowd, the Europeans headed into the singles matches on Sunday leading 9-7. The sun made a welcome appearance after two damp, overcast days and the galleries increased substantially with the prospect of another great European victory.

The opening match between Ballasteros and Azinger set the tone for the rest of the day, with unnecessary quibbling and posturing. Both players served up some outstanding golf and Azinger won it dramatically on the 18th hole 1-up. The Americans got it back to 9-9 but, as the matches played out, all eyes were turning to O'Connor and Freddie Couples, who were both playing their second match of the week. They came to the last tee all-square, with Europe needing only two points to retain the Cup.

Jacklin describes what happened:

> On the 17th green I got a strong sense that Freddie's stroke was somewhat tentative, probably due to the tension. Freddy is normally so relaxed you feel he might fall asleep out there. He is loose and carefree, with a very easy demeanour. There was something suspect about that stroke. I may have been wrong; perhaps that's what I wanted to see.
>
> In any case I caught up to Christy as we walked to the next green. Stay focused, I told him. I don't think he's quite right. Even if I was wrong I knew that Christy would take heart from this.
>
> The 18th at the Belfry is a long formidable par-4, with water curving in and out down along the left side. Longer hitters can carry it far enough to eliminate a good chunk of the hole. Christy was a good striker of the ball but not particularly long off the tee. He hit a

decent drive, leaving him with a long approach to the green.

Freddie pulled the shit out of his drive but his length enabled him to carry his ball out into no-man's land – a little peninsula. It wasn't what he had in mind but he got a break because his ball found a dry lie. This set him up nicely for an 8-iron to the green which was a bread-and-butter shot to a player of his skill. To say I was worried at this point would be an understatement. If Freddie got up and down it could have been game over. I was walking the fairway with Christy, trying to convince him that the hole was his to lose even though he had a long 2-iron to the green.

I invoked everything I could think of: 'Listen to me Christy. Just knock it on the green. Something good is going to happen. Come on. Just one more good swing for Ireland.' I can't believe I said those words and I can't say if they had the desired effect. What happened next would go into the folklore of the Ryder Cup.

He struck that 2-iron so sweetly and so pure I wonder if he even felt the contact. It flew to the green and stopped six feet from the hole. This was putting it up to Freddie big-time. He was clearly rattled now and he hit an abysmal 8-iron that veered way right of the hole. The rest was history. It was a massively important point, given that, surprisingly, some of our big guns didn't play their best that day. Freddie and Christy shook hands and that was that. We'd won it again. Through a tie, yes, but the Cup was still ours.

The celebrations that followed were tempered by the failure of the Europeans to gain a half-point for outright victory. Brand, Woosnam, Torrance and Faldo were defeated in their matches. The Americans could take heart even in defeat; their fight-back was resolute and they battled for every point, providing a memorable finish.

'AH CHRISTY, THAT'S THE SHOT. DIDN'T YOU ENJOY THAT?"
How did Junior react to all this excitement swirling around him? He
didn't need any exhortation from Tony Jacklin. When you have the
most influential figure in both your personal and you professional
life walking the fairway with you how could you not be confident?
'Himself', Christy Sr, was on hand at a crucial time and not for the
first time. To those who know what he meant to Junior, it came as
no surprise.

Senior filled the void when his brother John, the nephew's father,
died in 1985. Junior became much closer to the older man, confiding
in him, listening to him. Christy fitted into the younger man's family
life seamlessly in his natural, easy way. This was possibly the most
important contribution that he made to Junior's life. He didn't do a
bad job in terms of golf either.

For years O'Connor Jr was overawed by the ability and accomplishments of his uncle. How could he even approach the stature of the
great man? It was a daunting task and of course he was always going
to be compared to him, reasonably or not. As the younger O'Connor
began to make his mark he commanded the respect of his uncle.

> I achieved a major breakthrough when I won the
> Carroll's matchplay in Kilkenny in 1973, beating
> Jimmy Kinsella by 3 and 2 in the final. That was when I
> discovered for the first time that Christy believed in my
> ability: he had backed me to win. I only discovered this
> when the tournament was over; it was unquestionably
> the biggest lift of my life.
>
> It did wonders for my confidence and from then
> on, I availed of every opportunity I could get to play a
> practice round with Christy before a tournament. His
> message to me was always the same: timing. And when
> I got it right, he would say: 'That's lovely. That's what
> you want.'

And that's what he got on that 18th tee in the Belfry.

He couldn't have been more supportive. 'You're playing fantastic,' he said to me in the practice ground. 'You're hitting the ball magnificently,' he went on. And I knew he was right. That gave my confidence a massive boost because I knew Christy was not in the business of making idle comments, just to give me false hope. 'Swing the club,' he urged.

Those words were still ringing in my ears as I stood over that 2-iron shot on the Sunday against Freddie Couples – turn your shoulders and swing. And when it was all over, Christy paid me a lovely compliment. 'My God, I can't believe you made such a full follow-through on that shot,' he said. He was a great man to spot the quality in a shot.

It took me back to those times when I'd be hitting balls close to the hole and he'd shake his head and say, 'That's not you.' But when I got a real, solid strike, even though the ball wouldn't be as close to the hole, he'd say: 'Ah Christy, that's the shot. Didn't you enjoy that?' That shot often came up in conversation in later years during those special times we had together in my house in Clarinbridge.

6

RONAN RAFFERTY:
A MODERN-DAY JIMMY BRUEN

Ten years ago, Ronan Rafferty was Europe's number-one golfer. By the end of the current season, he may well have lost his Tour card.

Just what is it about Ronan Rafferty? He's on the brink, doesn't know if he'll ever be a serious competitor again, and nobody seems to give a damn. One of Ireland's finest and once the best in Europe, his game has died and there's no requiem…no eyebrows raised in surprise that such a talent could fall so low. Rafferty is forgotten.

Not that he gives a curse. While he was winning seven tournaments in Europe, playing in the Ryder Cup and making himself one of the world's best players, Rafferty never courted popularity.

Mark Jones, the *Sunday Tribune*, 9 July 2000

The career of the legendary Jimmy Bruen has been well chronicled. In 1936, while still a pupil at Presentation Brothers, Cork, he won the British Boys' Championship. He was viewed as the natural successor to the American Bobby Jones before the war, until a wrist injury curtailed his career. Bruen was seventeen when he won the 1937 Irish Close title. He then clinched his place on the winning Walker Cup team in 1938 with a sensational double in that year's Irish Amateur and Irish Close events.

Almost forty years later Ronan Rafferty captured the attention of the golf world. He was inevitably regarded as the new golfing prodigy when he followed up on his victory at the British Boys' Championship in 1979 by winning the Irish Close and the English Amateur Open the following year at the age of sixteen. Rafferty would be ranked in the top six of the greatest players and prodigies in Irish golfing history, along with Joe Carr, Jimmy Bruen, Cecil Ewing, John Burke and, of course, Rory McIlroy.

Rafferty's attenuated career is a most compelling story. He was one of the most explosive talents in the world of amateur golf prior to joining the paid ranks at the age of seventeen after the 1981 Walker Cup. He lived up to his reputation as a 'can't miss prospect'. In 1989 he sensationally won the Volvo Masters at Valderrama, the final event of the season, to top the European Order of Merit. He played in the 1989 Ryder Cup. The 1989 season would be the pinnacle of his golfing life.

In contrast to Rory McIlroy, who began his professional career in whirlwind fashion, Rafferty's initial foray into the paid ranks was humiliating:

> I had been a Walker Cup player, Eisenhower Trophy also and Irish champion. I was full of confidence going into the Tour school at Quinta Do Lago in Portugal. By my reckoning, if I broke 75 four times, the world stage awaited me. It had been a few years since I shot over 75.
>
> Well as it happens, I played four rounds (77, 79, 74, 80), including 80 on that last day, and missed my card by a single shot. To say I was shocked would be an understatement. More than anything, I was embarrassed. There were no press conferences or interviews. 'Boy Wonder No More – No Card,' summed it up.

Rafferty was forced to try another route to the European Tour; this took him to South Africa to compete on the Sunshine Tour. If he could finish in the top fifty in their money list he was eligible to play on the European Tour. 'Like everyone at some time,' he says, 'I had to bite the bullet and off I went to the Southern Hemisphere for the winter with my tail between my legs.'

His confidence was dented but he was still young, with that hint of arrogance that would become his trademark. His sponsors believed in him, a shrewd decision as things turned out. He left Ireland in November with no card and his first European Tour event was planned for Easter week in Tunisia.

Over the next four months on the Sunshine Tour Rafferty's talent and determination stood to him. He achieved his target with little to spare but enough to gain him entry to the European Tour event in Tunisia. 'Feelings of embarrassment were replaced by happiness and confidence that I could return to winning ways.'

His rookie season on the European Tour saw him finish forty-eighth in the European rankings. The highlight of the season was his maiden victory in the Venezuelan Open. Achieving that first win as a professional was a huge confidence-boost to the young Rafferty: 'Any great player will tell you that the first victory is by far the most important. It gives you belief to move on. In Venezuela I beat a field which included several big names including Andy North, the two-time US Open champion.'

The next seven years were consistent if not spectacular. This changed dramatically in 1989, when he had two victories to his name going into the final event of the season, the Volvo Masters. His putt on the final green was remarkable and ranks with the all-time great strokes under pressure. Rafferty picks up the story:

> Jose Maria Olazabal and I were head-to-head for the Volvo European Order of Merit title. On the 18th green, I was faced with a putt of five feet across and down the hill to win both the tournament and the number 1 crown. Words can't describe the feeling when I saw it go in.

Nick Faldo was already in the clubhouse on 283 and Rafferty needed to par the closing hole to pass the reigning Masters champion. That dramatic par was a lucrative one. Rafferty secured a £66,600 first prize and a £65,000 Volvo bonus for topping the Order of Merit. That season's earnings of £400,000 moved him past the then magical £1 million-mark in career earnings. He was twenty-five.

THE BELFRY 1989 (BRABAZON COURSE)

This was a Ryder Cup with a difference. The Europeans, captained by Tony Jacklin, were returning to Europe as Ryder Cup holders.

Rather than taking offence at Raymond Floyd's unwitting insult, Jacklin used it to motivate his team. 'Talk about having it handed to you on a platter,' he would later say. 'I didn't need anything else to motivate my guys.' This European side included Ballasteros, Nick Faldo, Bernhard Langer, Christy Jr, Sam Torrance and Ian Woosnam.

Europe had a 2-point lead over the Americans heading into the Sunday singles. Rafferty drew Mark Calcavecchia. Calcy and Hubert Green had defeated Rafferty and Langer in the opening foursomes, 2 and 1. In the Saturday foursomes the same pair defeated Rafferty and Christy O'Connor Jr, 3 and 2. The players seen enough of one another over the first two matches and the animosity was evident.

Calcavecchia didn't like Rafferty's attitude; neither was Rafferty too impressed with the reigning British Open champion. Calcavecchia is one of the PGA Tour's most popular players. He is friendly with Tiger Woods. He's a bit of a prankster and battled his share of physical ailments. No surprise that he and David Feherty would in time become great friends.

In the 1987 Ryder Cup, Calcy played in only one match in the first two days. When Jack Nicklaus told him on the driving range on Saturday that he would not be playing in that day's matches, Calcy burst into tears. He is an emotional man and his passion for Ryder Cup play runs deep. In the Sunday singles he confirmed this by defeating British Open champion Nick Faldo 1-up. Thus began an American rally that wasn't quite enough.

In 1989, Calcavecchia – who had also been victorious in the Phoenix Open and Los Angeles Open – and Rafferty matched shot for shot until they reached the 18th hole. The Americans won three of the first four matches – they were not handing the Cup to their opponents on a platter, as Jacklin would have it.

Calcavecchia's drive on the 18th hole went into the water; so did his second. He conceded the match to Rafferty, walked to the green and sat with his team-mates. He pulled the visor over his eyes and cried inconsolably.

Two years later he would blow a 4-hole lead over Colin Montgomerie and halve the match on the final hole. He says:

> I had enough tension at Kiawah Island [South Carolina, 1987] to last a lifetime. What happened to me was damaging in a way. It was something I'll never forget. Two successive Cups and disaster on the 18th. The first [against Rafferty] was a loss and the second was even worse. It felt like a defeat.

The matches ended even at 14-14 and Europe retained the Cup. Rafferty's only Ryder Cup appearance was a successful one.

Rafferty was overlooked by Bernard Gallacher for the 1993 Ryder Cup.

> I was somewhat surprised because my form was good heading into the autumn with four top-ten finishes and I was victorious in the Austrian Open. One is always affected by these disappointments but I'm philosophical about these things anyway. Maybe the fact that I had missed my tour card the first time round made it easier to accept. I wasn't devastated.

Rafferty grew up in Warrenpoint, County Down, where Don Patterson was his early mentor, coach and friend. Patterson was a big part of his early development.

Rafferty attributes his shortened career to the amount of golf he played, even with injuries, starting with his earlier days.

> I was playing well ahead of my years. Scratch at fifteen and +1 at sixteen. I played for the Irish Boys' team and my club at senior level at the age of fourteen. The following year I was playing for my country at the top level and for Great Britain and Ireland. I know I was way ahead of my time. But my professional career has been hampered only by injury.

As his golf career was interrupted by injuries, Rafferty turned his attention to other interests. Most noteworthy were his golf travels. Although technically a full-time player, he still travelled to hundreds of golf courses playing golf for fun. He also developed an interest in fine wines, having invested his earnings wisely. He has an impressive wine cellar; he has become very knowledgeable and will share a bottle with friends. He's not a wine snob but he clearly enjoys talking about his well-established interest.

'Typical, isn't it?,' says Feherty:

> He's the last guy you'd expect to have an interest in the gargle…sorry… fine wines, is it? What a waste of good booze. Too bad I was in America drinking my noggin off while all this was happening. I would have taught him a thing or two about my favourite fine wine, which was actually Jameson, the rare stuff.

Asked to summarise his career, Rafferty says:

> I missed out on my youth but it was definitely worth it. I have been lucky throughout my career. The school I attended had a good golf team. Also, Warrenpoint had a tradition of producing excellent players and the club was used to success. My parents were wonderful

and would drive me to events, although I was probably driving them round the bend.

I was blessed with everything and by everybody and I was able to find competition away from my local course. For me, that was vital. I'm grateful to have had that opportunity as a young golfer.

7

Philip Walton: What Price Success?

The most peculiar pairing in the Irish Open at the start of the new millennium brought together Philip Walton and Ronan Rafferty, the two finest Walker Cup players of their generation, full of promise and can't-miss prospects for the professional game. By 2001 they might reasonably have been a formidable double act.

Sadly for them, they were only bit players in a game that had passed them by. In 1985, few would have envisaged that Walton and Rafferty would lose their playing privileges and be dependent on invitations and sponsor exemptions.

Where did it all go wrong for these two considerable talents?

The question is particularly appropriate in the case of Philip Walton. Rafferty, as we have seen, succumbed to injury. The precipitous decline of Walton is a cautionary tale about the alluring life of the professional golfer and the very fine line between success and failure.

The root of Walton's decline can be traced directly to his winning putt in the 1995 Ryder Cup. Four years after that he lost his playing card and he believed that the melodrama associated with the singles win over Jay Haas had a lot to do with his slump. 'Just think of all the guys in that team who have played poorly since or given up altogether,' Walton says. This observation is worthy of investigation. What made the 1995 Ryder Cup so damaging and life-changing? This is the subject of a compelling book by American golf writer Tim Rosaforte, *Heartbreak Hill, Anatomy Of A Ryder Cup* (1996).

Walton was the lone Irish representative in the European team that contested the 1995 Ryder Cup matches at the Oak Hill Country

Club in Rochester, New York. The European team was not lacking in diversity, with Langer from Germany, Woosnam from Wales, Faldo from England, Sam Torrance from Scotland, Per-Ulrik Johannsen from Sweden, Constantino Rocca from Italy and Ballasteros from Spain.

The European team was captained by Bernard Gallacher and his American counterpart was the formidable Lanny Wadkins. This time round the European travelled by Concorde, which was considered extravagant in some quarters but reflected Gallacher's attention to detail. A veteran Ryder Cup player, the Scot ensured that every comfort and convenience was put at his team's disposal. If nothing else, Concorde's arrival added a touch of glamour and excitement to the city of Rochester and its airport.

Before the Europeans arrived in America there was intense media criticism of their selection of players and the prevailing consensus predicted defeat for a team devoid of superstars. The 1995 matches witnessed the intrusion of the media to an unprecedented level, putting added pressure on the players to perform. The Ryder Cup had become the most significant golf event in the world. But it came at a cost: the circus-like media attention overwhelmed the last vestiges of the purity and sportsmanship of the event.

Lanny Wadkins selected what became known as his 'dream team' – they were supposed to be a sure thing and defeat wasn't contemplated. As expected they led the first two days' matches by a substantial 2-point margin This was the first time since 1981 that the US team had the lead on a Saturday night and the Europeans were 1-6 in singles from that point.

The Americans were ahead 9-7, needing only to win five of the singles matches to take the Cup. For many observers the lead seemed insurmountable; it would take something near-miraculous for the Europeans to prevail on Sunday. The singles matches served up a roller-coaster emotional ride for players and spectators alike. When it was all over, Oak Hill was aptly named Heartbreak Hill. More than hearts were broken on the final day.

'No matter how hard the press beat me up, I deserve it. They won't be any harder on me than I am on myself,' Curtis Strange said after losing to Nick Faldo in match 24.

This was a demoralising defeat for the Americans. Strange, a controversial captain's pick, could have won the match with a par at the 16th but failed to hit the green with a 6-iron. The two-time US Open Champion finished bogey-bogey-bogey. At the 17th hole Faldo pulled even with a par-save.

He won the match with what he called 'a 4 to remember' at the 18th.

Strange left the course in shock and disbelief. His alleged cast-iron swing had deserted him when he needed it most. He was inconsolable; he blamed his loss for the Americans' defeat. In time he would come to terms with what had taken place but he was never the same player again, confirming Walton's observation.

With Faldo's defeat of Strange, Europe took the lead for the first time, 13½-12½. In match 25, Torrance defeated Loren Roberts 2 and 1 and immediately behind them, Corey Pavin defeated Langer 3 and 2.

Match 27 was Philip Walton against Jay Haas.

Walton recalls:

> Heading out for my match with Jay Haas, I had no indication that it would turn out to be the deciding one. I suspect he felt the same way. There was an unspoken admission about that the matches would be decided earlier. After all, the Americans were leading by two points. A gambling man wouldn't have bet against that team not getting five points from twelve matches.

With two matches still on the course, there was a despairing hope among the Americans that Jay Haas, Strange's old teammate at Wake Forest University, could save the day for them. This was a big ask, as Walton had Haas dormie. On the 16th hole, Haas holed out from a bunker for a birdie to a rousing cheer; there was a faint glimmer of hope.

If Haas could halve his match with Walton, the US might get out of jail, as Mickelson was leading Per-Ulrik Johannsen. That would leave the teams at 14-14, with the Americans retaining the Cup. If Haas failed to get a half, the last match would be of no consequence.

At the 17th hole, Haas hit one of the best iron shots of his career. From two hundred yards out, under branches, his ball came to a stop fifteen feet below the hole. Walton responded with a typical links bump-and-run shot and the ball stopped four feet short, leaving him with an eminently possible putt. That he was using a long-handled putter – an indication for many that the player is not entirely confident in his putting – was not lost on the American spectators.

Haas was first to play and studied the line of his putt from every conceivable angle. There was a pronounced silence: the only sound came from the blimp's whirring motors over the throngs surrounding the green. Fifteen feet. If he made the putt the pressure on Walton would have been all but unbearable. He missed. The ball never touched the hole.

Four feet and the victory goes to Europe.

Walton missed.

Despair for the Europeans: a glimmer of hope for the Americans. The sun was shining and the afternoon was comfortably warm for the spectators in Rochester.

Walton was oblivious to the conditions; what he did have was a heightened sense of the magnitude of what had taken place and what might lie ahead:

> I realised when I missed that putt how important our match was. The crowd in the stands went totally wild. I couldn't see the end match on the scoreboard, because there were people standing there and there were heads blocking it. Sam Torrance came up as I walked through the crowd and said, 'C'mon, you're still one up!' Then I realised: this is it.

Haas had won the 16th and 17th holes with a birdie and a par. With one hole remaining, he needed to win and make the crucial half-point. 'It was a madhouse, absolutely crazy,' Haas recalled. 'How were you supposed to play golf under these circumstances? I know that Philip had similar thoughts.'

Haas had not played the 18th hole in the matches but he remembered it from the practice rounds. 'I didn't like that hole in practice and here I was faced with having to make a par and hoping that Philip might come up short.'

The 18th hole at Rochester is a 445-yard par-4. Haas drove first. 'I don't like the sound of it,' said Johnny Miller in the broadcast booth. Haas had popped it up, a disastrous drive at the worst possible time, that ended up deep in the trees. Worse still was the lie, with no easy way out through the branches and tangled undergrowth.

Walton fared a bit better, hitting a weak slice into the right rough. More crucial however, his ball came to rest on a good lie.

> It was just a nerve-wracking experience. I went back to the tee and people were right behind me, close enough to touch me. I could feel the hair standing on the back of my head and then my right leg started shaking. It wasn't my favourite tee shot all week anyway. I was trying to squeeze the thing down the left side and it just moved on me.

There was a lot of confusion, with the marshals trying to move the gallery. This gave Haas more time to consider his options. In truth every way out had a downside – playing a draw or a cut or just laying up were all perilous.

Walton's situation was relatively straightforward: he knew his yardage and had a metal wood in his hands.

Haas finally went with the hook, drawing a shot into the fairway. Walton immediately hit his shot, landing it on the bank short of the green. From there the worst he could make was bogey. Haas had to get it up and down or it was over.

From close to a hundred yards Haas was not able to hold the ball on the green and it ended up on the fringe. What should have been a routine wedge-shot for Haas had turned into another atypical error. Haas was widely considered to be one of the best wedge-players on the Tour. 'All I wanted to do was get it to ten feet. I wish I could have that shot over,' Haas said later.

Walton was down by the bank; the grass was deep and he did not immediately find his ball.

> I nearly walked on it. I was halfway up the bank and I thought to myself, 'Hold On,' and as I stopped I looked down and there it was between my two feet. One of the spectators said, 'Hey, did you walk on it?' I had a feeling I was pretty close.

Walton faced an uncommonly difficult shot; playing out of the deep US Open-style rough was unfamiliar to him. During the practice rounds Ian Woosnam showed him how to make this type of pitch. It required a deft touch, dropping the club on the ball and hoping it came clear of the rough. 'It looked like the ball wasn't going to clear,' said Johnny Miller. 'It was so close to hanging up.'

The ball cleared the bank, opening the door for Walton:

> I just didn't want to get it above the hole. From the back to the front of that green is treacherous. You can have an eight-foot putt and run it fifteen feet past.

Haas ran his chip shot six feet past the hole; he may have over-compensated by not wanting to leave it short. Walton was left with two putts from twenty feet straight up the hill, a mere formality. 'I've got two putts for it,' he told his caddie, Bryan McLauchlin. 'I think I'll take them.' He lagged up to two inches, the putt was conceded and victory went to the Europeans. He was immediately hoisted (rather clumsily) into the air by Bernard Gallacher, who shouted in his ear, 'You've just won the Ryder Cup.' According to Torrance, 'Philip, ever one for the puzzled expression, looked surprised.'

Walton himself said:

> When I was playing that last hole it felt like I was never going to get to that green. Flying home on the Concorde it began to dawn on me that I could really have messed up on the last hole. Over the putt itself, my concentration could not have been better. On the plane, on the other hand, I suddenly started thinking: What if I do something crazy over this putt?...What if I whack it miles past the hole and mess things up for everyone?

This delayed irrational fixation points to the stress Walton was under. When the pressure is this extreme, one has to question the worth of a Ryder Cup that seemed to have lost everything it was supposed to represent. 'It's getting almost too much to bear, this Ryder Cup,' said Bernard Gallacher on the 18th green.

Ballasteros concurred: 'There's too much pressure, too much pressure. People don't realise how much pressure Jay Haas was under.' Because Walton emerged victorious, there was a mistaken assumption that it had been easier for him, adding to the mythology surrounding the Ryder Cup. The following years would bear this out: Haas got his career back on track; Walton was never really the same player again.

The Europeans had silenced their critics. To get 7½ points out of 12 was a considerable achievement. It was not the best European team: Olazabal was missing, Ballasteros was a shell of the once great player and Faldo was in the tabloid headlines at every turn.

Over two thousand people had been at Rochester Airport to greet the arrival of Concorde a week earlier. On Monday, perhaps twenty showed up to see the Europeans depart.

The first stop for the European team three hours later was Dublin Airport. As the Concorde came into view before landing it was raining hard. The roads leading to the airport were jammed for about ten miles with cars flashing their headlights. Five thousand people, including An Taoiseach, John Bruton, showed up at the airport to greet the team. The first man out the door of the Concorde was Philip Walton; he was carrying the Ryder Cup.

When Walton holed the putt that won the Ryder Cup he became the first man in history to do so with a broom-handle putter and in the process completed a clean singles sweep for the men with the long sticks. Mark James and Sam Torrance won their singles.

'Philip might have been using a curling iron for all he knew,' Sam Torrance said. 'He seemed almost unaware of the situation, although that was probably just his little-boy-lost look.' Torrance was on the right track. There was certainly something lost on that final green but it wasn't Walton's boyish looks.

THE INFLUENCE OF JOE (J.B.) CARR

Philip Walton was one of Ireland's greatest amateurs of the modern era. The honours he accrued as an amateur were comprehensive: He played for Great Britain and Ireland in the Walker Cup in 1981 and 1983; on each occasion he won 3 points out of 4. He was the Irish Amateur Champion in 1982 and a full Irish international between 1979 and 1983.

The influence of J.B. Carr on several leading amateur players cannot be overestimated. Carr was the quintessential match-play golfer with an unshakeable self-confidence. He imparted his knowledge and experience to many of the players who were fortunate to play for him. He took amateur golf to a new level and got better treatment for his players. His aim was to have his players feel better about themselves and play with enhanced pride and confidence.

Philip Walton's relationship with J.B. Carr was typical of that enjoyed by all the amateurs who were associated with the legendary figure. Carr thrived on challenge and met it with utter confidence and conviction. It was ironic that Walton, one of his star players, would lose the vital ingredient that had enabled him to scale the heights of Ryder Cup glory:

> Joe Carr was the first guy who really got the Golfing
> Union of Ireland to spend more money...he was way

ahead of his time and his whole attitude was very positive. I got on well with Joe but he was a tough nut.

The Walker cup team was tough to make. I was only nineteen but I had to go and prove it to myself. He advised me to play in a couple of tournaments and said that if I did well he'd support me in whatever way he could. I'm grateful that he took me under his wing. He was pushing all the time and I went over to the Scottish Strokeplay on his advice and won it that year. Joe Carr helped me a lot!

FORGOTTEN HERO

Walton reached the apex of his professional career in the 1995 Ryder Cup. The man who had won the French Open and the English Open (both in a playoff) went into a gradual decline and eventually lost his playing privileges. He persisted courageously and won his card back but ultimately his career as a contending professional golfer was finished. The platform for great success that the Ryder Cup victory should have provided for him did not materialise and the best that he could manage was 'the prison sentence of Tour School'.

There are a number of reasons for this dramatic fall-off. 'For seven years after the Ryder Cup I thought every day I might never make it back,' he said after coming through the Tour School in 2004. 'As you keep missing cuts your confidence goes down and the stress builds and builds. You get caught in that cycle and it wears you down in every way.' Des Smyth points to another factor:

Tiger Woods dragged the young guys to a new level. Montgomerie was doing it in Europe and Tiger is doing it all over the world. They are setting up the courses tougher and tougher, yet if you shoot 71 or 72, it just doesn't rank.

POSTSCRIPT: THE CHAMPIONS TOUR 2008

Jay Haas returned to Oak Hill Country Club this year and quieted some demons on his way to a spectacular win in the Senior PGA Championship. From the left rough of the 17th hole on the famed east course, Haas hit a fortunate shot in Round 3 that propelled him into contention.

> I won't say that it won the tournament for me, but it certainly got me in the mix. I was sitting on the 15th green, five strokes behind, and playing 16 and 17. I'm tied for the lead. I didn't have to shoot 68 on Sunday to win.

Haas, the 2006 Senior PGA Champion, holed an improbable 8-iron from 162 yards for an eagle 2. He held off Bernhard Langer by 1 shot with a 7 over-par total, the highest final-round score by a champion since 1980.

'That was pretty miraculous,' Haas said of his 8-iron shot that landed well short of the green, bounded into and out of the first cut of rough, made a left turn and rolled into the cup. It was no surprise that ESPN [the US sport network] made the shot its 'Play of the Day'. And it reached a global audience in the days that followed. 'I could stay out there a long, long time and never do that again. It was just a freakish thing.'

The win, cemented by a par at the 72nd hole, also served as a personal redemption of sorts for Haas. The memory of the loss to Philip Walton is still vivid in his memory – same hole, major pressure but different outcome this time around. Haas said:

> I had a little chuckle to myself on the 18th tee. It was like, 'You've been talking about this. Time to put up or shut up. You talked a good game, about just getting up there and ripping it.' Damn if I didn't do it. Did it make up for what happened in 1995 against Philip? You don't make up for those shots, they stay with you. But it sure as hell was very sweet when I crushed that baby out there today.

8

Feherty and Torrance:
'The Song Remains the Same'

To gauge the magnitude of what the Ryder Cup has become over the last two decades, listen for a moment to a reflective Sam Torrance, a successful Ryder Cup player and the winning Ryder Cup captain in 2002:

> For the first time, three Irish players qualified for the European team and achieved a remarkable victory at the Belfry. That doesn't begin to explain the passion surrounding this biennial tournament.
>
> Since 1973, the Irish have punched above their weight in the Ryder Cup, providing some of its defining moments. That 2002 Cup was no different, except that Harrington and McGinley, two of my dad's (Bob Torrance) star pupils, were on the team.
>
> The week was young but old enough for me to have a run-in with my dad. He had asked for a buggy to go out with Harrington and McGinley to offer a few hints and last-minute fine-tuning. A precious commodity in Ryder Cup week but I was able to find him one. Off he went as happy as a guru with a camcorder, while I finished breakfast and did some thinking.
>
> When I ventured on to the course, I saw him and the buggy in the middle of the fairway, parked about five yards behind McGinley. This was a steam-rising

rather than gasket-blowing situation.

'Dad,' I said as I approached him. 'You can't park on the fairway.'

'Come here,' he said.

'What?'

'Come here,' he repeated.

I wandered closer to him.

'Fuck off!' he whispered, 'I've waited forty years for this moment.'

'Okay, Dad, carry on,' I said.

That day Bob Torrance drove where he wanted. By the end of the week Paul McGinley made the winning putt, adding another Irish chapter to the folklore of the Ryder Cup. I finally understood what my dad was on about.

The incident was tacit acknowledgement and approval from a father proud of his son's golfing accomplishment. Sam Torrance's whole golfing career was somehow crystallised into that one moment for, in truth, Torrance, who won thirty-two times around the world, had left one or perhaps two British Opens slip from his grasp. His captaincy of the Ryder Cup team that week was the defining moment of his career and is what he will be remembered for.

I might have been a better player but I wouldn't have been as happy. I would love to have won the Open and the Order of Merit, but apart from that there's not much I haven't achieved.

An American player with my record would have played over a hundred Majors. I've played thirty-odd British Opens and a handful of American ones. The British Open was just the be-all and end-all. It almost did get too much for you because it was the highlight of the year, the thing you looked forward to.

There's not the same sociability nowadays in

European golf. We had an absolute ball. It was a great way of life and great fun, especially when a bloke by the name of Feherty was involved. I'm still fond of a few pints after a round to take the edge off and relax.

Let me tell you about Feherty's experience because he probably told you a pack of lies, the swine...

When David made the 1991 Ryder Cup team he was anxious to know what it was like.

'It's like having a kid,' I told him.

He came back with one of his smart responses: 'But I never had a kid and when did you give birth?'

'Listen, my boy,' I said to him. 'You cannot explain to someone who does not have a child what it is like having a child. That love, that feeling, is hard to explain and it's the same with the Ryder Cup.'

I think that may have registered with him but he kept needling me. 'When did you have a baby, Sam?'

This is the same guy Americans came to know and love many years later. We were very close in those days and of course Bernard [Gallacher] put us together.

Our first outing was in the afternoon fourballs against Lanny Wadkins and Mark O'Meara. My God, Feherty was nervous. He was ghostly-white, if that's possible. His first putt gave me a scare. It was about fifteen foot and finished three feet short and four feet wide of the hole. He actually came close to missing the ball, hitting the ground in front with his putter head. By now he's starting to turn green, several shades of green.

I put my arm around him. This was my sixth Ryder Cup in a row and I thought that might help him, you know – the old dog and all that. I was rolling a cigarette as we walked to the second tee. I slowed down a bit and I said to him, 'You're on the same team as Seve, Faldo, Langer, Woosie and Monty but most important of all, with me!"

'Aye, that's true enough,' he said sheepishly.

'Now then,' I said taking a deep drag of the Old Holborn and blowing smoke in his face. 'You'd want to be enjoying it, like. Or if you want to be a prick about it I'll be joining Wadkins and O'Meara and you can play the three of us guys.'

That got his attention.

He settled down eventually; It may have been due to the smoke I blew in his face. On the second nine he began to play fantastic stuff. We came from 3-down to take the match to the 18th. Feherty was left with a ten-foot birdie putt to halve the match. He asked me to read the line. 'Left edge, Just knock it in,' I said firmly. Sure enough he did. I was immensely proud of him although I didn't tell him that at the time. I knew then he would give a good account of himself no matter what way the rest of the matches went. I wonder what he told you about that day. I still say a pack of lies...the swine.

FEHERTY REMEMBERS, CIRCUITOUSLY

I had the perfect preparation and qualifications for my eventual Ryder Cup début. When I was in school I spent most of my time looking out the window, blissfully indifferent to what they were trying to teach me. The only class that got my attention was Geography. I loved it when the teacher pointed out different places on the globe. And to prove to us imbeciles that the world was round, he would spin this globe with a flourish. Now that's what you call a life-lesson.

When I was fourteen I remember going with my dad to the Double Diamond ('Drink the Beer that Men Drink') Tournament at Gleneagles. My golfing heroes, Bernard Gallacher, Brian Barnes and all those guys, were there. And then there was Peter Alliss, a formidable golfer and Ryder Cup player in his day. Peter and Henry Longhurst were the soundtracks to my childhood. That was back in the days when we were meant to lose the Ryder Cup. Even our best players were getting beaten. Okay there was one exception in 1957 but that was before my time. It still counts as a rare win but I would love to have been there.

Feherty spent two years as assistant to Fred Daly at Balmoral, Belfast.

Those were the two greatest years of my life. Fred was one of the funniest men I ever met. When you're working in a pro shop earning fifteen quid a week, there's a lot of low moments but Fred was such great fun. I would have paid him for the privilege of being there. It was fabulous.

Daly won the British Open at Hoylake in 1947 and he finished runner-up to Henry Cotton the following year. Once he told Feherty: 'You know my game is just as good as it ever was, although I don't hit the ball as far. One thing that bothers me is that I can't get out of the bunkers like I used to.'

'Well,' said Feherty, 'have you tried these new 60-degree wedges?'

'It's not the ball I can't get out,' retorted Daly. 'It's me.' Daly was gregarious and quick-witted, with an outrageous sense of humour that got him banned from Balmoral several times.

'He had the bearing of an idiot savant,' Feherty remembers fondly. 'He wasn't so much a golf teacher as a player who taught by feel.'

Giving a lesson to the renowned amateur Garth McGimpsey one day, Fred became frustrated, seized the club and hit three perfect 7-irons as a demonstration. Still, Garth failed to grasp what was obvious to Fred.

'You're not watching,' he said, marched over to a grass bank and began chopping at it with the club. 'See that?' he cried, 'See that?'

'See what?' asked a bewildered McGimpsey.

'See that moss,' Fred told him. 'That's what's been killing our greens.'

There are so many memories, stories and wonderful times. One day I asked him for advice on my backswing, which had become so long I could see the club out of the corner of my left eye. We went into the car park and I made a few practice swings.

'I know what you should do,' Fred said. 'Close your left eye.' In other words don't change a thing. He was fond of a G and T and drove a Hillman Avenger, in what might be best described as a 'babyshit orange'.

Anyway, back to the Ryder Cup. Feherty continues:

When they changed the format of the Ryder Cup to a Europe versus USA tournament it was only a matter of time before it became a meaningful contest. Mind you, we have to thank Ballasteros for the early success. Seve reinvented the Ryder Cup. He breathed life into it. When it became Europe it became Ballasteros. He was the catalyst, the driving force. He was such an enormous figure in the game. He saved the Ryder Cup; the tournament was dead after the beating we got in 1981, even with the Europeans.

In Palm Beach Gardens, for the 1983 Cup, there wasn't even national TV coverage and nothing close to national media attention. The Europeans might have won that year; playing the last hole Wadkins (yes that same guy) hit a sand wedge to a foot from the pin and the Americans won 14½-13½. Wadkins told me that Jack Nicklaus, the American captain, went out to the fairway after his shot and kissed the divot. I think Wadkins had it bronzed, or he should have the way he still goes on about it.

Seve was at best an acquaintance of mine; we may have played a few times together. I wouldn't have numbered him among my close friends. I'm sure he felt the same way about me. I tell you he was more than a close friend that week.

One of my most extraordinary memories of the Ryder Cup was the Kiawah set-up; it was part of a new development and there was no clubhouse, just two trailers. The parking lot was crowded with these mobile homes because there was nothing built. Seve was everywhere giving back rubs, massages, encouragement.

We had quite a few rookies on that team: Paul Broadhurst, David Guilford, Richardson and myself. 'You nervous, Heferty?' Seve'd ask. He drove Tony Jacklin nuts too, always calling him Mr Hacklin. 'You not worry, Heferty, me shitting in the pants too.'

He made me feel bigger; in a peculiar way he made all of us feel bigger by making himself smaller – if you follow. We were a bunch of no-name players who were, perhaps understandably, underestimated by the Americans. That edge is gone now; we don't have it any more.

There was no question about who I wanted to play with. It had to be Sam: he was my best friend, drinking buddy and just about everything you would want in a friend. I don't think the pairing did a lot for his Ryder Cup record.

We went out in the afternoon pairings and I played kind of shaky all day. What Sam told you was correct but it was actually worse than that. Sam told me to let the Americans go first so that they could hear the applause for us. Great strategy for Sam and experienced players but I could barely get the tee in the ground.

And as for that first putt; it was six feet short and eight feet to the right. When I stubbed the ground in front of the ball with my putter, I remember Sam saying, 'Pull yourself together or I'll join those other two guys and you'll have to play all three of us.' That was how tense the atmosphere was and I reckon Sam must have got me to settle down enough to get around.

Ours was the last match of the day and it turned out to be pivotal. We got an important half-point and somehow I made a crucial putt on the 18th hole. Sam read the line of the putt, told me in no uncertain manner what to do and it went in.

I was drawn against the late Payne Stewart in the Sunday singles matches. At that stage, I'd been through every possible emotion imaginable during the week and I was beyond fear. I didn't care who I played; I felt as if I could beat anybody. Payne was a great friend of mine, a great guy and a notorious practical joker.

One year down in Houston, he put a groundhog in my room. Took it straight from the boot of his car, supposedly dead, while I was out on the course. When I got back to my room and opened a closet there was the groundhog wearing a pair of my underpants. I no longer wear underpants; you can figure that one out for yourself.

I found myself 4-up with four holes to play. Just behind our pairing, Mark Calcavecchia, who later became a good friend, was in the process of tossing away a 5-hole lead to Monty. In the meantime, Payne won 15 and 16 against me, the bastard, leaving me 2-up with two to play.

On our way to the 17th tee it was mayhem. A tunnel erected for the players to go through collapsed and there were people all over the place. We had to push and jostle our way through and a big lady marshal jumps in front of me, pokes me in the chest and says, 'Just where do you think you're going?'

She thought I was a spectator trying to sneak through. I was about to lose it at that point. Next thing Payne put his arm around me, chewing tobacco with that shit-eating grin on his face and says, 'Ma'am, I believe he is playing against me,' and he swept me up on to the tee. A lot of players would have walked past, knowing that I was about to lose my temper and possibly the match. Not Payne Stewart. He was passionate about the Ryder Cup and knew its history. Besides, he was my friend. Taking advantage of a situation like that wasn't how he operated. Remember it was Payne who conceded that putt to Monty at Brookline [1999], after he had been so badly treated by American fans. Monty blamed me for that too but that's another story.

Payne struck another wonderful shot at the 17th but I matched it. I knew my ball was headed for the heart of the green. Bernard Gallacher was going around with his arms in the air. Tony Jacklin was still looking the other way with his hands over his eyes! The match ended there and Payne was gracious in defeat. He was a terrific sportsman. Not only that – he was a gentleman in the best sense of the word.

All the flak he took emanated from people who didn't know him or understand him or who he was. Anyway, they were the sort of people he didn't want to let know who he was. His tragic death left a hole and it's still there.

That was my one playing experience of the Ryder Cup. I had qualified for the team quite early on in the year, which was a surprise. A couple of other years I might have made the team but didn't.

I loved every minute of it and I hated every minute of it at the same time. That's the sort of player I was. Nicklaus says he thrives under pressure. Tiger says he loves it when the pressure is on. Me? I hated that shit. I wanted it to be over.

There's comfort in mediocrity but there's no comfort in having to be the best. I was never comfortable, always squirming like a toad. That's probably why I played my best golf in team contests – the Dunhill Cup, the World Cup. Whenever I had mates around me I seemed to play better, for some reason

I even tried a mixed doubles event once with Laura Davies [UK]. We spent most of the time at the dog track somewhere in Florida. It was mid-November, after all.

The Ryder Cup has always been important to the players; even when the Americans were winning, they took great pride in representing their country. It was their only chance to do so. It was also a wonderful social occasion and to me that's the one regret.

Now there are press conferences, autograph sessions and compulsory memorabilia signings and players are paraded a bit like a dog and pony show. Of course this was inevitable. It's a huge earner and every opportunity is taken to maximise this. But something gets lost as a result.

Sadly, the teams don't mix any more. They are cut off from each other with all their respective obligations. Quite a few of the players from both teams don't drink at all. Perhaps that's not a bad thing.

After the matches were over, Sam and I went into the US trailer. It was fairly bouncing around and Dan Quayle was in the middle of some speech and we just broke up in laughter, much to the delight of many of the American boys. We had friends in there and it seemed the logical thing for us to do. We got horrifyingly drunk that night.

I vomited on Lanny Wadkins's shoes, which he's never forgiven me for. He had a pair of alligator loafers; he was always very dapper. I'm not convinced the players of this generation have similar memories. Lanny and I talk about those days all the time. I wonder if the players of today enjoy the Ryder Cup the way we did?

Europe lost in 1991 but certain moments remain vivid. There was the putt that Bernhard Langer missed on the last hole and the memorable picture taken of him bent over backwards in agony as the ball slid past the hole. The photographer was a great friend of ours and Bernhard too. He approached Bernhard in the trailer and put his arm around him and said, 'I can forgive you for the putt but I can't forgive you for the six million Jews.' Talk about context any way you like it!

Europe is enjoying a tremendous stretch of wins because we are playing better than the Americans. It's swings and roundabouts and the Americans are going to get their share of wins. There's no doubt in my mind about that. It's still kind of a surprise when the Europeans win, a nice surprise, though.

RONAN RAFFERTY

I played a lot with him. We were second in the World Cup in 1992 and 1993. The Germans won it. Bernhard Langer was playing with a guy called Torston Gideon, obviously the second-best player in Germany. We knew him well; he was a great guy and the only other German player on Tour.

There was one great moment. The matches were

played at Grand Cypress in Florida. You had to stand with your national flag at the opening ceremony. Rafferty looks at Torston and says, 'What are you doing here?

Torston replied, 'I'm sorry. I don't know what you mean.'

'Well, I thought they would have left Bernhard play twice.'

I'm standing there cringing and thinking: what a thing to say! Here's a guy representing his country for the first and maybe the only time in his life.

I turned to Rafferty and said: 'You bollix, what a thing to say.'

'Ah, I was only joking.'

As it turned out we ended up playing with him in the last round. Torston shot a 65 and Langer also played quite well. Rafferty didn't play particularly well all week and the Germans won it. Torston made shots from all over the place; he played inspired golf.

As we shook hands on the last green, Torston says to Rafferty: 'That's what I'm doing here.' Just brilliant. He waited four days to deliver one of the all-time great comeback lines in golf.

I shouldn't be so hard on Rafferty; he was a wee bit younger than us. Of course there was nothing malicious in it. Bear in mind he was a Warrenpoint boy, a club with a tradition of producing excellent players.

He developed in an environment where success was expected and he did partner myself and Philip Walton when Ireland won the 1990 Dunhill Cup at St Andrews. Rafferty was a massive talent, long before massive became part of the sporting vernacular. Christ, I hated him for being so talented. On the other hand, his career was wrecked because of injuries to his hand and he never realised his potential.

EDDIE POLLAND

My memory of Eddie has nothing to do with the Ryder Cup but it has plenty to say about Eddie. In 1979, I was at Lytham Green drive trying to qualify for the British Open. Eddie was out there as well and he got himself into a playoff. After the usual preliminaries an announcement was made by this ancient red rosette-wearing old boy with impeccable public school enunciation.

'Is there a Mr Poland, Puland...the playoff will commence shortly. I say, is there a Mr Pewland, Roland, Buland...' This goes on for a few minutes before Eddie realised they were looking for him.

Eddie gets up in the man's face and declared, 'My name is *Polland* and you'd better learn how to pronounce it because I'm liable to win this thing.' I was an assistant at Balmoral, the only club with three Ryder Cup representatives – Fred Daly, Polland and myself.

DES SMYTH

The Irish have been very influential in the last twenty-five years of the Ryder Cup. A big part of that can be attributed to the role played by Smythy as a player and later as an vice-captain. I knew him well from the early Tour days in Europe: a great guy, a sweetheart.

PADRAIG HARRINGTON

They say that Harrington was the second Irishman to win the British Open. He most certainly was not; he was the first. You wouldn't have called Fred Daly Irish; he was an Ulster Unionist. Padraig should win a few more Majors; he's got the stomach and guts for it, which means everything.

DARREN CLARKE

Darren's story has been well documented but I'm still sweet on him both as Ryder Cup player and on an individual level. His time is coming and he's got to take it in the next few years. He also has the mind to do it and I thought he'd be the first to win that Major. He is certainly the most talented of them all.

Clarky's a throwback, an anachronism. He's the reincarnation of Walter Hagen crossed with Tony Lema and a rhino. Talk about a breath of fresh air! Darren's biggest problem is Darren. Sometimes he gets in his own way. When he is bad he is dreadful but when he is good he is unbeatable. Don't ask me why. You might not want to ask him either! Maybe it's an Ulster thing, you know. We have that bit of a glitch.

9

Fleeting and Not-So-Fleeting Madness

A few ugly minutes overshadowed the 1999 Ryder Cup at Brookline, Massachussets The Americans staged a remarkable comeback; their players understandably over-reacted to Justin Leonard's putt, and golf etiquette was temporarily breached, although not permanently scarred. The American writer, John Updike, penned his reactions to what happened that Sunday afternoon in an article called 'Back to Brookline' in *Travel and Leisure Golf* (September 2004). It is a heavily nuanced piece, sensitive, romantic, tinged with no little nostalgia, beginning, 'I was a marshal at the 1999 Ryder Cup matches.' Updike is a golfing enthusiast and has written extensively about the game.

> ...A fellow marshal and I stood on the seventh tee, keeping an eye out lest the vacated hole fall victim to turf thieves and we saw on the distant screen a misty enlarged ball dart into a giant hole and a group of men in homely brown shirts, recognizable among them Tom Lehman and Tiger Woods, mob Justin Leonard.
>
> What had happened? 'We must have won,' my companion said. I was happy to hear it. But why, then, as the minutes passed, was Jose Maria Olazabal squatting down on the cleared green so solemnly? He was sizing up his putt. We had not won; he was putting to tie the hole. The Teletron showed our foe's putt running up the slope and missing by a few inches to the left.
>
> We had won. Glory be.
>
> The spontaneous and slightly premature celebration

of Leonard's forty-five foot miracle putt was much deplored in Europe and indeed it was a breach of golf manners as they used to be. The Ryder Cup matches got our blood up and is this altogether good? One of golf's charms, surely, is its suppression, under traditions of civility and good humor, of the competitive rawness that has made for example, European football riot prone, North American (ice) hockey cruelly brutal and professional tennis a mêlée of grunts and ungracious gamesmanship. In recent years the Ryder Cup matches have been sullied by disputes over money (the players get none), Padraig Harrington's slow play (is it deliberately aggravating?) and captain Seve Ballasteros's buzzing about in a golf cart at Valderrama exhorting his troops like a Little League coach on speed. Does the Cup make golf blow its cool? An us-versus-them fervor belongs to less companionable, less meditative, less cosmopolitan sports. It's not as if these foreign golfers don't live, many of them, in Florida and Texas, their wives swapping recipes with ours. The players dress in the same locker room and share the same swing doctors. Unilateralism, triumphal or not, sits awkwardly on a sport whose fickle, quirky difficulties form a great leveler. The essential contest in a golf round exists between the player and the course...

WHAT HAPPENED?

What happened, does anybody know?
What happened, where did America go?
I remember the morning the towers fell
I fell back asleep and I dreamed of hell.
Merle Haggard, 'What Happened?'
The Bluegrass Sessions (2007)

David Feherty was deeply affected by the sudden violence and death of 9/11. He was a young man when the Troubles in Northern Ireland broke out. That violence did not prepare him for the devastation in Manhattan that changed the way we live. Feherty, long regarded as golf's quintessential funny man, is in reality a profoundly humane individual, sensitive, insecure and vulnerable. His recall of these events clarified his vision of mankind and defined his compassion for the inadequacies of the human condition. It will take its place alongside the finest and most enduring pieces of golf writing.

It's all too easy for those of us who are lucky and good enough to make a living from professional golf to forget that we live in the real world. Lots of money, perks like courtesy cars, free meals and equipment, plus the adoration of fans, create a cocoon of privilege and a sense of invincibility. But soon after the 1999 Ryder Cup was over, our perfect existence was shattered, not once but twice.

One month after Brookline, Payne Stewart died in a private jet crash. It hollowed out all of us in the world of golf. It could have been any one of us in that little Lear but Payne Stewart was more than a little different. He was so familiar, so touchable and so loved that millions, inside and out of golf, were drawn to the TV screen, watching the fateful jet inch across the screen again and again like a ghastly CNN video game. It couldn't happen but it did and it left a smoking crater on the landscape of golf that can never be filled. And there was no event in which Payne Stewart's character shone through better than the Ryder Cup. More than anything in his career, he loved to play for his country.

The second awful reality check was the horror of September 11, 2001. Growing up with troops on the streets of Ulster, with the carnage of frequent bombings and sectarian murders in the news all the time, it shouldn't have affected me as badly as it did the average American but for me, it might have been worse. This wasn't supposed to happen here, not in the land of the fresh start. This place was exempt from the kind of religiously-driven insanity that boils up and suppurates out from centuries of evil, cruelty and intolerance-in-the-name-of-God, over in the old countries. But suddenly, the stench was upon us and the whole world reeled, for despite what anyone might have heard or read about anti-American sentiment, America and the American dream is much loved throughout this little planet. But people don't write letters of commendation, only complaint. Countless millions, perhaps billions, still dream of living in this amazing place and to see it violated in such a way was utterly horrifying. It still hurts to think about what happened and why and to see how our world has changed – living in fear, many of our freedoms challenged and knowing that the world we're leaving our children is not as safe as the one in which we grew up.

Nothing was immune from the aftermath, including the Ryder Cup, which was to have been played a little more than two weeks later in England. With the teams picked and ready to go, the decision was made to postpone the matches for a year but otherwise change as little as possible: the teams and the venue would remain.

If there was some good to come out of the tragedy, it was the washing away of the bad blood from Brookline. After September 11, 2001, fighting would be reserved for something more important than a golf match between rich men in bad shirts. There was no room for hostility among friends. Sport thrives on competition: one side will always lose and the other win. But more than ever, we needed to remember that what we're doing was not life and death and that when the games were through, we could sit together, have a drink and laugh.

But it was a shitty way to be reminded.

Opinion was sharply divided on the question of going ahead with the Ryder Cup. That golf must not give way to terrorists was strongly argued in some quarters. This was a reasonable argument but playing two weeks after 9/11 was never likely to happen. No sporting event was affected by 9/11 quite as profoundly as the Ryder Cup.

'A great opportunity has been lost, as trivial as it is,' Feherty told this writer:

> If ever there was a time to return the Ryder Cup to the way it should be – a great rivalry played in the right spirit with respectful fans – this was it. I think we would have seen great golf. The Americans would have been given a fantastic welcome, absolutely no crowd trouble…the playing of the national anthems, the European players holding little American flags. I could see the whole thing before me. It was perfect but it was just not to be.
>
> The decision to postpone was the right one, indeed the only one under the circumstances. If anyone tells me that golf or indeed any sport is a microcosm of life, they should take a step to the left. Sport is a microcosm of nothing. The American players are family men and when you consider the enemy that's out there, it made sense to stay home. These terrorists, they're lovely people, aren't they? They'll hide their children beside them and they enjoy watching their own people die. They're not part of the human race, as far as I am concerned. They have abdicated their responsibilities and forfeited their right to be treated as such.
>
> It's positively asinine to suggest that the Ryder

Cup teams should change, simply because the event was postponed. The date is immaterial; this is the 2001 Ryder Cup. If they played it forty years from now and half the players were in bath chairs and needed ear trumpets, they still should be playing one another, no one else. Some of them will play only once. To rob anyone of what is one of the most special moments in a golfing career would be a crime.

As for the three Irish in the top fifty, I think we might be set for a great era in Irish golf. I'd like to see more of them over here too. It'd give me something to crow about. Harrington played great here last year, should've won. I'm sure he will too, as he's at least as good a player as Westwood. Clarkey has already proved he has the nads for it and McGinley is the sort of player who'll dart in and steal something every now and then. Reminds me of me without the big gob.

10

THE END OF THE AFFAIR

It's difficult to pinpoint exactly when David Feherty and Colin Mongomerie had a much publicised stand-off, falling-out or perhaps no more than a simple misunderstanding. Its origins are unclear but it spanned two Ryder Cup events, starting after the 1999 event in Brookline and coming to a happy ending after the Belfry contest in 2002.

Colin Montgomerie is a complex, fascinating man. David Feherty once famously described him as having 'a face like a bulldog licking his own piss off a nettle'. This comment did not help the relationship between the former Ryder Cup team-mates and it was taken out of context and used by others to insult and anger Monty.

In the spring of 2000, Mark James, who had been he Europeean captain in 1999, published *Into The Bear Pit,* in which he divulged team-room secrets and delivered a strong attack on the US team for their behaviour at Brookline. In the book, James referred to an awkward scene in the European team-room at Brookline. James had invited Feherty to join in the post-match festivities but Colin Montgomerie took exception to the Irishman's presence. According to James, Montgomerie wanted Feherty ejected from the team-room, so James had a word with Feherty, who left and went to the public bar. This was an inaccurate account, as Feherty explains:

> I've taken my fair share of digs at the big man (as I do
> at everyone) and sometimes they've missed their mark,
> wounding him deeply, for Monty is a sensitive soul with

issues he'd rather keep to himself. For these, I'm truly sorry. Colin Montgomerie will always be a hero of mine.

Unknown to his readers and admirers, Feherty was gutted by what was essentially a misunderstanding. When he put on his public face there was laughter and hilarity; beneath the laughter were tears of despair combined with consumption of dangerous levels of Bushmills.

Feherty recognises the essence of Montgomerie's personality.

> He's soft and there are always a few who are going to play on that. As usual it's not what happens to you that counts. It's how you respond to how what happens to you...
>
> The fact is the vast majority of the people out here want to love him beause there's an embraceable human frailty to him that other players don't show. His big mistake was being hurt by it all. He's not a very outgoing person; he won't punch the air and salute this and that. That's seen as rude over here but it's not meant to be. It's just the way he is.

Several hours after the startling American comeback and victory in Brookline, Feherty went to join the European players.

> I walked from the Copley Plaza over to the Four Seasons for a few drinks with the boys, hoping that they weren't too devastated by the loss. When I got there I found the usual mixture of sadness, regret, disappointment and promises for the future.
>
> It's safe to say there was a good amount of drink consumed. All the players to a man hugged me; Monty was the salient exception. He was nowhere to be seen. I had stayed away from the team all week, not wanting to upset him during the matches as I knew he was having

a hard enough time of it. I recall his wife Eimear telling me at a pre-match cocktail party that she would never forgive me for what I had done to him.

Monty was still in his room, devastated after a heroic effort. The rest of the boys were dealing with the disappointment in their various ways. James was being his philosophical self while his wife Jane was threatening to kill anyone who wasn't European with a furled-up umbrella. In walked Monty. His look spoke volumes. He was in a purple mood. He stood in front of me and said, 'What are you doing here? You have no right to be here.'

I waved around the room and said, 'Monty, I'm a Ryder Cup player, just like you. There are plenty of us in here.'

Monty just stormed off past everybody, back to his room, with his head down.

James was staring at the ground. I'm not sure what Torrance was doing but it was clear to me that I had to go. Monty deserved to be in that room with his team-mates and I knew that while I remained, he wouldn't come back. I made my apologies to all present and wove my way back on to the streets of Boston.

I was heartbroken. It's funny how certain moments stay with you. I found an empty Budweiser can and with my hands in pockets, kicked it all the way back, into the lobby, up the elevator and into my room at the Copley Plaza, with tears streaming down my face.

The magnitude of what Monty had been through weighed heavily on me. He put up with all kinds of ugly crap that week and still managed to play outstanding golf. I sat on the bed and I knew that no matter how badly I was feeling, it was worse for him. And I had been partly responsible for his misery. I still have that beer can.

Feherty would have to wait until the 2002 match at the Belfry to make his peace with Mongomerie. In the intervening two years the intrusion of violent death on a massive scale undermined certainties, even in the relatively insular world of golf.

Europe's 3-point victory in the 2002 competition did not surprise Feherty.

> The team line-ups for the singles matches were questioned and the wisdom of Curtis's decisions were heavily criticised, very unfairly I think. The truth of the matter was that it didn't matter what way the pairings matched up. The cumulative emotion and history that Sam had in him filtered down to his boys. Sam's team simply wanted to win more and was going to, no matter what.

The Europeans were collectively 24-under-par on Sunday versus 7-under for the Americans. Shortly after victory was assured came the best moment of the day for Feherty.

> It was thrilling theatre, astonishing golf and just as exciting as the Battle of Brookline but with almost none of the spite and no bad behaviour. The crowds behaved and there was little or no heckling. Best of all for me, Sam [Torrance] led the incredible war-horse Montgomerie over by the hand and put him in front of me. Monty smiled the biggest, warmest smile I've ever seen, threw his arms around me, lifted me off the ground and I got to thank him and tell him that no matter what he'd read or heard, he'd always been a hero to me. Finally, after the débâcle at Brookllne, I got a hug from the one brother I needed most. He'll never know how much it meant to me, or to Sam.

11

PETER OOSTERHUIS AND JACK NICKLAUS: HONORARY IRISHMEN

Never you mind about his nationality, sunshine. Was Fred Daly Irish? Oosty happens to be a good mate of mine, and, not coincidentally, one of the all-time great people on the planet. He's a star in every sense of the word and I can say without hesitation he'll gladly give you what you need. If you've nice, not naughty, I'll have him ring you in the New Year. You can include him as an honorary Irishman.

David Feherty (December 2007)

When you get a reaction like that it becomes very easy to include Peter Oosterhuis among the Irish. He was a frequent competitor in Ireland in the 1960s. Okay, so I'm bending the rules a little here because again 'Feherty said so':

Oosty played his last Ryder Cup in 1981 and, like Jack Nicklaus, he finished with twenty matches in six years. The big dude's record of 14-11-3 was especially good for someone who'd endured some of Great Britain's worst years. He would go back to the US and struggle on the PGA Tour, where he had only one victory, the 1981 Canadian Open.

In 1977 after going 3-0 at Lytham (including a foursomes win with Faldo over Nicklaus and Watson), the big lad said, 'I don't understand it. Here I am beating the top Americans, yet for the rest of the year I'm struggling to stay in the top sixty.' There was a simple answer, though. Oosty was a Ryder Cup player, one of those who really got it bad. To be on that team meant so much to him that he was able to find something deeper within him, the courage to attack and find out how good he really could be.

And he was good, believe me, a lot better than some gave him credit for. Most players can't bring themselves to grasp the nettle, some touch it in individual events, but Oosty saved his best for the six Ryder Cup teams on which he played. The big guy should captain a European team soon, whether or not he lives in America – no one deserves it more.

Peter Oosterhuis played on six Ryder Cup teams 1971–81 and was undefeated in seven matches. He says:

> The Ryder Cup has been the perfect stage for sub-elite European players to make the headlines. More often than not, an Irishman was in the thick of it and that never surprised me given the depth of amateur golf there and the tradition of matchplay. The format in the Ryder Cup is often the great equaliser.

Oosty is a dispassionate observer of a game he dominated in Europe for several years in the 1970s. For four consecutive years, 1971-4, he won the European Order of Merit, a record that endured until Colin Montgomerie's seven-in-a-row (1993–9).

> The money in modern golf is extraordinary. Yet, I was staying in nice hotels, travelling with a small child and nanny. I had a nice car and didn't think I was missing anything.

> When I was winning those Order of Merits, I made
> a total of £68,000. When Colin clinched his fourth, he
> made £2.4 million.

Oosterhuis laughs at the disparity:

> Oh, I have no regrets about playing in that era. What's the
> use? It doesn't do me any good and I never think about
> money differences unless reminded by others.

He has fond memories of his first Ryder Cup (1971) when he enjoyed some heroics of his own. The match was played at Old Warsaw CC, St Louis, Missouri.

> I played against Gene Littler, one of my heroes, and
> Arnold Palmer. We had two series of singles in those
> days. Palmer played all six matches and to be fair, he
> was very tired when I teed up against him. After four
> or five holes, I knew I had an excellent chance to beat
> him. It was a huge physical struggle for him.
>
> Six rounds in three days is draining, so I beat him
> handily. He was in his early forties and still an excellent
> player. He won two or three times on the US Tour that
> year and there I was, a mere twenty-three years old,
> without a clue as to how big a name Palmer was. It was
> only later that I realised the real meaning of it all but I
> can't say that I beat him. He was in no shape physically
> to play that last round.

Oosty beat Palmer comprehensively at Muirfield, Scotland, two years later (1973) by 4 and 3.

He was at Valhalla commentating for one of the major US networks and is frequently on the Golf Channel, Sky Sports, Canadian TV and the BBC. His final word before the start of the 2008 Ryder Cup was : 'Prepare for the unexpected.'

JACK NICKLAUS: THE GREENING OF THE GOLDEN BEAR

When Tiger Woods prepares for the Open, almost invariably he heads for the rich pastures of the Golden Vale in County Limerick to stay with his good friend J.P. McManus. This provides Tiger with excellent preparation and he also manages a bit of fly-fishing for salmon and trout in complete privacy.

Tom Watson is strongly associated with Ballybunion and was made honorary captain there. He too recognised the value of preparation over the famed Kerry links for his forays to Britain for the Open and he has been actively involved in the reshaping and building of a number of greens.

In recent years, more and more high-profile American players tune up for the Open in Ireland. The late Payne Stewart was an annual fixture at Waterville. After playing several practice rounds in Lahinch, Phil Mickelson declared it 'the finest links course in the world'. He's not far off the mark, although a case can also be made for Portmarnock, Ballybunion and several other links. Thus far Mickelson has not claimed the famed Claret Jug but he may well do so before his career is over.

Decades before these visits, one man became very familiar with Ireland, its people and Irish golf. This man was none other than Jack Nicklaus. This association goes back to the days when a career as a golf professional was not particularly lucrative.

Nicklaus, with characteristic modesty and self-effacement, was never one to boast of his association with golf in Ireland. For many golf fans his link with Ireland is the American-style course he designed in Mount Juliet, County Kilkenny.

Jack Nicklaus is perhaps the most thoughtful and authoritative commentator to be found on any aspect of golf. He introduced the power era to golf, built the first stadium course, Muirfield Village in Dublin, Ohio, where the 1987 Ryder Cup was held, with Nicklaus the American captain. Courses built by Nicklaus Design are found around the world. Nearly four decades ago, he played an intregral role in the creation of the PGA Tour.

The survival and subsequent growth of the Ryder Cup owes

much to the vision of Jack Nicklaus. He plays down his role:

> Golf fans everywhere want to see competitive rivalries, matches, tournaments. There is an argument to be made that the Ryder Cup is now too serious, that it has drifted from its original aims. It's emblematic of the game's growth all over the world. Who could have foreseen that?
>
> When the Ryder Cup is played in the spirit in which it was meant to be played, there is no better sporting rivalry. My one wish is that the Ryder Cup should be played in the same spirit as the President's Cup [US against the Rest of the World]. Just let the players go play golf. That's my opinion. And that's why I enjoy being US captain for the President's Cup.
>
> I captained two Ryder Cup teams [1983 and 1987]. It's a great honour for me to do that. Being captain is something I enjoy and it's a great thing for the game of golf. We do what we have to do to make sure that it's a competitive event, that everyone enjoys it but you also try to get the bragging rights at the end.

This prompts Nicklaus to reflect on the legacy of J.B. Carr.

> I know the satisfaction it gave J.B. to see his teams winning. He took players under his wing and taught them how to play, to compete and how to behave. He was passionate about matchplay golf. He wanted Irish guys to qualify for Walker Cup teams. And quite a few of them have gone on to become successful professionals and ambassadors for their country and the game. He was a huge influence on the amateur game in Ireland and brought an air of professionalism to it. He treated his team guys well.
>
> I think his legacy goes beyond the game of golf.

We both played golf in a great period. Great, enduring friendships were made. J.B. was first and foremost a family man. His family was far more important than any golf game. I understand that now more than at any time in the past and it also applies to my own family.

J.B. was a believer in being a part of family life, part of the community and part of things that are going on. For him, life wasn't just about playing golf.

There's more to life than playing a game, particularly (in my case) when you don't play that well. J.B. approached the game in a professional way but he held fast to the amateur ideals at all stages of his life. What more can I say about a good friend.

12

DARREN CLARKE:
THE TRIUMPH OF ACHIEVEMENT

By nature, professional golf is a selfish game, utterly selfish. When you are out there, you are trying to beat everyone else, you're trying to beat your best friends. There are some fantastically nice guys on the Tour and you have to enjoy the feeling of beating them. If you are a professional golfer, the simple economics of it say that you have to beat other people to survive.

Darren Clarke

When Darren Clarke became the first European to win a World Golf Championship event, beating Tiger Woods in the Accenture 2000 36-hole final, his reputation was considerably enhanced in the States; he had finally arrived on the American scene. Clarke was indifferent to the euphoria surrounding this victory. He explains:

I never worry about that kind of thing. I tell you, though, I've had a very mediocre two seasons by the standards I want to set. I expect to win tournaments, Majors included. It was very frustrating because I worked very hard on all aspects of my game but the results didn't show it. Aye, it was a great win surely, but my focus had always been on the Majors. There is definitely unfinished business there.

Shortly after holing out to win the World Golf Championship, Clarke was approached by David Feherty of CBS. 'This is a moment that I have looked forward to,' said Feherty, before asking a few questions of the Big Fella. 'I suppose you will have a wee dram to celebrate tonight?' Feherty asked. Clarke smiled broadly. 'I'll probably have one…or ten,' he replied.

Programme scheduling did not allow for any more questions. Nonetheless, in those few moments, Clarke demonstrated why he was so hugely popular in America. Said Clarke: 'I think they [Americans] see this big Irish guy walking down the fairway smoking a cigar, or trying to cadge a cigarette from a caddie, looking as though he is having a nice time and they are fine with that.'

When Clarke returned to the locker room after beating Tiger Woods, there was a surprise in store for him. Scrawled on his locker was a note from Woods: 'Congratulations. Be Proud. PS You're still a fucker.' Curiously, to that point in his career, he had not connected with his Irish fans to the same degree. That would change dramatically in the space of a few years.

Clarke had been labelled as an under-achiever, enigmatic, hot-tempered and lacking in the desire to do what it takes to win. Those close to him knew a different person, a man driven to succeed but who could relax and enjoy life away from the game. There was a maturity in the way he went about his business.

One of the first to see the change was Butch Harmon, his swing coach:

> I had my doubts about him. He seemed to be in a comfort zone or something and he was going nowhere. I was infuriated because he is one of the most naturally talented players I have ever worked with.
>
> He worked hard on his game and showed a willingness to make a few key adjustments. I didn't believe that he would ever again be a real factor in the Majors. He had opportunities and I thought maybe they had passed him by. Well, that has certainly

changed and he is now back among he game's elite. I see no reason why he won't go out and win a Major in the next year or so.

In 2003, Clarke took the first-round lead in the Masters with a 66. Because of delays due to rain, the field had to play extra holes on Friday and Saturday. He posted rounds of 76 and 78. His weight and the soft ground took its toll on the Ulsterman and he resolved to do something about it. More sobering was the bout of breast cancer that put his wife Heather in hospital. She recovered from that episode but would succumb to the disease three years later.

Heather's first brush with cancer had a profound effect on Clarke:

> Sometimes, before, I let golf be the be-all and end-all of everything. I still have the same drive but it's not life and death. There are things a lot more important than golf.

In preparation for the 2004 season, Clarke shed more than three stone (47 lbs) and followed a structured fitness regime through the autumn. He said:

> There is the little business of the Ryder Cup again next year, and you really don't know what pressure, real pressure is, till you've played your first shot in the Ryder Cup. It's more nerve-wracking than the British Open, the Masters, anything. It never gets easy.

For Clarke it was never easy but his upbringing and background gave him a decided advantage when it came to matchplay. 'If you see you're playing him,' Hal Sutton said, 'boy you'd better buckle your chin-strap.'

Darren Clarke was born in Dungannon into a family with a long sporting tradition. His grandfather, Ben Clarke, was a professional football player for Sheffield United and his father Godfrey was also an accomplished player. Clarke played rugby in his schooldays as an open-side flanker and was known to his team-mates as 'Big D'. He was invited to an Ulster schools' trial at the age of seventeen but went playing golf instead. Golf was his first love: he 'got the bug' at an early age.

Godfrey Clarke became superintendent at Dungannon Golf Club when Darren was eleven. 'I got the bug for golf-caddying from my father. I started playing myself and couldn't get enough of it. In the summer I played seventy-two holes a day. I decided at an early age that I wanted to become a professional.'

Clarke, for the most part, taught himself to play on the course – there was no driving range or teaching pro – which enabled him to become a natural player. Simply put, he just stood up and hit the ball and by the time he was fifteen he was remarkably long off the tee.

It was then he discovered links golf and he and his father began making weekly trips to seaside courses. Royal Portrush was a favourite. His game benefited hugely. 'I love links golf, because you've got to use your imagination. You've got to work the ball, chip it, do everything.' His game took on added finesse with a deft touch around the greens.

America came calling when he was still a teenager, in the form of a scholarship to Wake Forest University, where Arnold Palmer played collegiate golf. It was a short-lived venture: Clarke quit abruptly after little more than a semester. 'The coach and I didn't really see eye to eye. We had a conflict of personalities,' he said. In truth, Clarke was more accomplished than some of the seniors and felt he should be playing with them.

It was a fortunate move by the youngster and he spent the next two years playing in all the big amateur tournaments in Ireland. Garth McGimpsey was the man Clarke looked up to at that time – and with good reason. Amateur tournaments provided an excellent foundation for matchplay:

> All the amateur tournaments when I was growing up were matchplay. That's why I got such a liking for

it. You see it's not always who plays the best golf but who can get it done coming down the stretch. The key is knowing when to attack and when to hit it in the middle of the green. I try not to get too aggressive.

It's very easy to try to force the issue early on to build up a lead. I've done it myself and it hasn't worked out for the best. So I try to hang about for a while and see how I'm playing and how my opponent is playing and just wait and measure it all up.

Clarke embraced sports psychology from an early age:

It was Arnold Palmer who said golf is 20 per cent physical and 80 per cent mental. I absolutely agree with the great man. You can have the greatest technique, the greatest swing and the sweetest putting stroke in the world but you'll never play the golf you're capable of if you have a poor mental approach.

When I was sixteen and had already decided I wanted to be a golf professional, I was introduced to the mental side of the game by the psychologist Peter Dennison in Portadown. After meeting with him my golf ambitions were clarified: I didn't want to be just an ordinary golf professional but a successful tournament winner. I have always thought a great deal about my mental approach to all aspects of the game – even before it became trendy – and am constantly looking to improve in that area.

I know Butch [Harmon] was very skeptical and used to slag me off about it. Butch is, dare I say it, old-school regarding such matters. Players and teachers can talk all they want: the thing about golf is you'll never get it right. It's the most frustrating sport in the world because you spend your time chasing perfection, yet you know full well perfection can never be found.

Perfection isn't a requirement to win a Major or to be a successful Ryder Cup player.

VALDERRAMA 1997

Clarke played on his first Ryder Cup team at Valderrama in 1997. It wasn't exactly an auspicious beginning but the Ryder Cup rarely lends itself to command début performances. Clarke, for all his talent, wasn't yet the polished performer. On the second day he was teamed with Colin Montgomerie in the fourball against Fred Couples and Davis Love III and they won by one hole. In his singles match against Phil Mickelson, Clarke was beaten 2 and 1. 'It was a memorable event because it was my first time playing in it. I didn't contribute a whole lot but we won,' he says. 'My performance was a bit ropy but I was out there against some of America's best. I also learned a lot from playing with Monty and I know it's a cliché but the experience would stand to me in later years in all competitions.'

BROOKLINE 1999

In the intervening two years, Clarke had become a more mature and formidable player and he played in all the matches at the Boston venue. He was still prone to fits of temper and moodiness when he wasn't playing well. 'He's very complex mentally,' says his manager and friend Chubby Chandler. 'But he got better and better as he got older and he began to understand himself. He used to beat himself up on the range for hours and if it was a bad day it would be hours and hours – he'd do it to make his hands sore.'

'I've learnt to deal with things better – not get as annoyed,' Clarke says:

> I can't affect what's happened before. It's not possible for me to play good golf through anger. Maybe for some people – I don't know – but certainly on my part no.

At Brookline, Clarke and Lee Westwood were teamed in the opening day foursomes and went down to Hal Sutton and Jeff Maggert 3 and 2. In the afternoon fourballs they beat Tiger Woods and David Duval by 1 hole.

On day 2, Clarke and Westwood defeated Jim Furyk and Mark O'Meara 3 and 2 but in the afternoon fourballs the Europeans were beaten by Phil Mickelson and Tom Lehman 2 and 1.

In the final days singles Clarke lost to Hal Sutton 4 and 2 and Lehman beat Westwood 3 and 2. Clarke says:

> Defeat at Brookline really hurt. Lee and myself volunteered to go out first and second in the singles because we were among the most experienced players. But it went wrong. Tom and Hal simply played better than us. How well the Americans had played in the singles was very much overlooked in the furore at the end.

Hal Sutton remembers that match:

> Darren was a sort of happy-go-lucky sort of guy but he was one hell of a tenacious competitor. I had him down in the singles and we were at the 9th hole. I had a two-footer to halve the hole and he made me putt it. As we walked to the 10th tee he said, 'Man, I'm sorry I couldn't give you that but in the situation we're in now, I just couldn't.' I would have done exactly the same thing if the roles were reversed. You couldn't but like the big fella.

It was clear that Clarke enjoyed the tournament, despite the startling European defeat:

> Lee and myself had a blast playing against Tiger and Duval. We were trying to win but that side of things can get lost. We had a great time telling jokes, all sorts of stuff. That's the spirit in which I think the Ryder Cup should

be played. Not all that other nonsense. And besides there was always next time at the Belfry when winning back the Ryder cup would erase the bad memories.

The match against Woods and Duval (world number 1 and 2 respectively) was significant for many reasons, not least of which was the high standard of play. Clarke made six birdies, including the one that gave the European duo its ultimate margin. He regards it as one of his best Ryder Cup matches.

> After a decent long drive, I hit a lovely wedge to the back tier of the 17th green, leaving a tricky-enough putt of about seven feet. Lee and I read the line and I stepped up and holed it. Looking at it later on video I saw was smiling as I was discussing the line with Lee. At the time I wasn't aware of that but I felt very confident.

After two Ryder Cup appearances Clarke's record was: played 7, won 3.

THE BELFRY 1992

Curtis Strange, the American captain, quickly set the tone for this match by sending Tiger Woods out with Paul Azinger. His intention was to get points on the board. Sam Torrance countered with Darren Clarke and Thomas Bjorn of Denmark. Clarke immediately set the pace and stole the show. His shot from the right-hand bunker on the opening hole was a majestic 8-iron 162 yards to eight feet and he duly sank the putt to give Europe the lead. He birdied 2 and 2. By the end of the match, he and Bjorn were 10 under par.

They beat the Americans – who were 9 under – by 1. Clarke would later say: 'Any time I get the chance to play against either with Tiger or against Tiger, it's always good fun. It doesn't matter who I'm playing, I'm going to go out and enjoy it.' Next to Woods, many shrewd observers regard Clarke as the world's most naturally gifted player.

First points to the Europeans began what was a Ryder Cup of sheer excellence. The afternoon foursomes saw Clarke and Bjorn lose to Hal Sutton and Scott Verplank, 2 and 1. In the Saturday morning foursomes the European duo lost to Woods and Davis Love III, by 4 and 3. This prompted Torrance to break up the pairing and in the afternoon fourballs, Clarke and Paul McGinley secured a half against Scott Hoch and Jim Furyk.

The Europeans headed into Sunday's singles tied at 8-8 and Clarke halved with Duval to secure an important early half-point. The overall result was a 3-point win for the Europeans with Paul McGinley's match-winning heroics against Jim Furyk.

Once again Clarke cemented relationships with professionals from both teams. David Duval credited Clarke with helping him to rediscover his passion for the game when the two spent the night drinking after the final day. That may well be but his wife's illness meant that Duval played only intermittently on the PGA Tour. Clarke also befriended Davis Love III as a result of playing Ryder Cup.

For Bjorn there was nothing but admiration for the Ulsterman. 'He has grown in stature and is becoming more and more of a leader in the clubhouse. A lot of us players look up to him and I can see his role in this area becoming even more influential in the future.'

OAKLAND HILLS 2004

The 35th Ryder Cup at Oakland Hills was an unmitigated disaster for the Americans. Under the quiet leadership of Bernhard Langer, the Europeans won 18½-9½. The Americans were out-thought and out-fought in every key area. It was a European team filled with heroes, none bigger than Colin Montgomerie. All twelve players got on the score sheet.

The rout began with Monty and Harrington beating Woods and Mickelson 2 and 1 in the opening fourball. The second match out featured Clarke and Miguel Angel Jimenez against Davis Love and Chad Campbell. This match gave Europe their first point with a 5 and 4 win.

As Clarke explained, 'We got some early momentum going and managed to keep it going.' Jimenez and Clarke cut quite a colourful dash. Said Jimenez: 'Well, we are both in the same mood, we like the same cigars…Cubans of course.' Langer expanded on this in his deadpan way:

> They both like wine. They both smoke cigars and they get on well with each other. I thought that was a good reason for pairing them together.

In the foursomes, Clarke teamed with pal Lee Westwood to beat Woods and Mickelson 1-up. The Europeans were 3-down after four holes and looked to be on course for a heavy defeat. However, a stirring fight back saw them 1-up after 11 holes and it was a tight affair until Mickelson sliced badly off the tee at the 18th, allowing Europe to edge home and pick up a crucial point.

On Saturday Clarke and Ian Poulter lost to Tiger Woods and Chris Riley 4 and 3 but in the afternoon, reunited with Westwood, the Europeans beat Jay Haas and Chris de Marco 5 and 4. Clarke played perhaps the day's outstanding shot when he hit a 6-iron to within a matter of inches at the 8th hole, to give Europe a 3-hole lead. 'We have complete trust in each other,' said Clarke. 'We know the other player has the game to do what has to be done.'

Sunday's singles began with Europe holding a 3-point lead. Clarke and Davis Love played a remarkable match of the highest standard. Love held the lead until the 16th where Clarke made a stunning birdie. On the 17th, Clarke chipped in from the back of the green to win another hole before seeing a four-footer for victory on the final green lip out. A half was a fitting outcome as neither player deserved to lose. Clarke was indifferent to the fact that he still hadn't won a Ryder Cup singles match.

> This is a team game. It would have been nice to get the win but you know what? We had a really good game, played in the right spirit. I'm disappointed about missing

that putt but Davis missed one there as well – and I think that was a very fair result for both of us.

THE K CLUB 2006

The long-anticipated and hugely-hyped 2006 Ryder Cup at the K Club did not disappoint. Darren Clarke would finally win a singles match in this his fifth Ryder Cup appearance. What he lost in the months leading up to the event will never be captured in any language or video technology.

On 13 August 2006 Heather Clarke died from breast cancer at the age of thirty-nine. For four years she had battled the disease in an unassuming and dignified manner. Her death was expected but for Darren and their two young sons that didn't lessen its impact. It's a chapter in Clarke's life that he has documented; the emphasis here is on his Ryder Cup play. 'I wouldn't want it any other way,' he says.

Once more Europe achieved an emphatic victory against the Americans. Their historic third consecutive victory in the competition matched the score of two years previously. It was a tournament of raw emotion, shadowed by recent deaths and shared grief.

Clarke's decision to make himself available to the team so soon after his wife's death was discussed and analysed. Clarke said:

> I did think long and hard about whether I should be here this week or I shouldn't be here and I came to the conclusion that I could help the team and benefit the team if I was here this week…I'm here, I want to play, I want to compete and I want to help my team-mates.
>
> I was desperate to be here but at the same time, if I didn't think I would contribute to the team and be a benefit to the team, I would have made the decision not to be available to play…with Tiger losing his father and Chris DiMarco losing his mum, there are more important things than trying to win this week. But in the end we're all professionals. We all want to win for our teams.

It was felt that Clarke might have an edge as he had played the K Club many times and indeed had shot a 60 en route to winning the European Open. 'It's a lot more difficult now,' Clarke conceded. 'Dr Smurfit didn't like it and changed it all around.'

After taking a 4-point lead into the final day, having won all four previous sessions over the Americans, the Europeans decimated the Americans in a sensational victory. It might have ended as a rout for the home side but a lot of nervy, tentative and unpredictable golf was played in the first two days. The variety of turbulent weather may have given the Europeans a small edge – especially those who had experience of its capriciousness on this course.

Clarke and Westwood combined to beat Mickelson and DiMarco by 1 hole in the Friday fourball. The following morning the same duo triumphed over Woods and Furyk by 3 and 2.

In the Sunday singles Clarke teed off in match 7 against Zach Johnson. An enormous, vocal gallery accompanied the two rivals. It was a tight match but Clarke reached the turn 2 holes up. The match swung in his favour on the long 10th hole, a par-5. Clarke drained a forty-foot downhill putt to go 3-up.

On the 12th hole the match was effectively ended as a contest, in dramatic fashion. Clarke putted from the edge of the green, perhaps a hundred feet, and found the hole. The crowd erupted. Johnson was stunned but battled back.

As they teed off from the 16th, Henrik Stenson secured the winning putt in the match behind. The Cup was staying in Europe and all eyes were focused on Clarke's match. When Johnson failed to birdie he conceded the match.

What followed was unprecedented; this kind of outpouring of emotion from the two teams may never be witnessed again.

The images of Tiger Woods, Tom Lehman, Chris Di Marco and Phil Mickelson, all finding their way to Clarke and hugging him in tears, was a timely reminder that the complexities of real life go far beyond any golf tournament. It was a defining spectacle: healing, cleansing, laden with sportsmanship, empathy and compassion – and ultimately brotherly love.

'What will survive of us is love,' wrote the poet Philip Larkin.

To live is to love and to love is eventually to lose one another or be lost to one another. Love and grief are inextricably bound. It is the universal unifying force, our fundamental vulnerability, our essential frailty, the ultimate demonstration of our humanity. This is the most vital and enduring image of the 2006 Ryder Cup.

COMEBACK

If Clarke had lost something of his game or of his desire to win after 2006, no one would have complained. His contribution to the game and to the Ryder Cup is immense. Within himself he knew there was more, and he resolved quietly and tenaciously to realise it. Clarke is a thoughtful, sensitive man. He can quote word for word a speech by Teddy Roosevelt. For him the speech basically says that even if you fail, at least you tried.

> It is not the critics who count: not the man who points out how the strong man stumbles or where the doer of deed could have done better. The credit belongs to the man who is actually in the arena, whose face is marred by dust and sweat and blood; who strives valiantly; who errs and comes up short again and again, because there is no effort without error or shortcoming; but who knows the great enthusiasms, the great devotions; who spends himself for a worthy cause; who, at the best, knows, in the end, the triumph of high achievement; and who, at the worst if he fails, at least he fails while daring greatly, so that his place shall never be with those cold and timid souls who knew neither victory or defeat.

Darren Clarke was forty when the 2008 Ryder Cup matches were played. His last significant win was in the 2003 WGC-NEC Invitational in Firestone, Ohio. It was a comprehensive 4-stroke win. After the 2006 Ryder Cup, questions were asked about Clarke's desire and ability to win, especially given his changed family circumstances,

After fifteen wins on the European Tour the questions, although inevitable, were misplaced. Clarke believes he has five good years left in him. In golfing terms he isn't old; there have been many Major winners well past the age of forty.

'As far as I'm concerned there have been a few people who have decided that I'm done but I wouldn't quite see it that way. I'm not quite bollixed yet.' As if to prove a point, Clarke scored a dramatic victory in the BMW Asian Open in Shanghai in April 2008. He had given himself a chance to play his way on to the Ryder Cup team. This was the indicative of the stature he holds. He was back in the familiar relaxed groove, striking the ball in an effortless, gifted way. He won again in Gleneagles later in the summer.

'It [the Asian Open] may not have been my biggest win but it was certainly the sweetest,' Clarke said at the time:

> I have proven to the world – and to myself – that I'm back. Throughout the dark days of self-doubt and occasional self-pity, I remained defiant that the golfing world had not heard the last of me. I didn't want to be remembered as a player who used to be successful. I'm not ready to concede on that for a while yet.
>
> My good friend Lee Westwood was a big help to me in this respect and was as supportive to me in my lean years as I was to him in his. But I've had a feeling all year that the days of beating balls for eleven hours on the range were due to pay off. And so it came to pass.
>
> Now I can start thinking that the world's top fifty is not beyond me. I may be turning forty this year but I'm not ready to throw it in. I am as driven as I have ever been. It's not too late to win a Major and that remains the prime objective.
>
> This would not have been possible without support of team Clarke. My boys, Tyrone and Conor, have been absolutely unbelievable in their support for me,

even though it has meant Daddy being away from home for quite long stretches. They have encouraged me to go out and play when golf did not seem to be as important as it once was.

Clarke is an avid reader and goes through quite a few crime thrillers on long-haul flights. He has a penchant for new cars: 'I change them far too often. I get bored with them very quickly and no matter how amazing or beautiful or fast they are, there's always something even more appealing.' His greatest treasures are, of course, his two boys. 'Apart from my boys, I still have quite a lot of bits and pieces from when Heather was alive. I've had our wedding rings joined together by a jeweller and that ring is very special to me.'

13

Paul McGinley:
'Sam' – Hoisting One out of Two

My real heroes were the Dubs – the Dublin Gaelic football team of the 1970s: Paddy Cullen, Brian Mullins, David Hickey, all those guys. As a kid I loved going to Hill 16 and my dream was that one day I'd be out there in Croke Park helping Dublin to win the All-Ireland and hoisting Sam.

On his putt that won the Ryder Cup:

This is really what it's about. We enjoy being tested. It's fun, and the bigger the test, the more fun it is when you succeed. It's not every week you win the Ryder Cup. All the lip-outs I'd suffered in the past just disappeared in that one moment. What a time to hit the best putt of your life.

I knew the putt; I had had the exact same putt in the Benson and Hedges at the Belfry the year before and I holed it. My caddy J.P. Fitzgerald kept saying that all I had to do was stick to my routine. I was very focused and motivated to hole it but the fear of missing was just as high. And then I looked up and it was about two feet from the hole, rolling straight for the middle...*wow*...it was like when a champagne cork explodes out of the bottle.

I'll never know what it's like to lift the Sam Maguire and bring it back to Dublin. To say it would be special is an understatement. But the feeling I got from holding up Sam Ryder's Cup for the European team was brilliant. One out of two isn't bad!

Jimmy Magee is known for his encyclopaedic recall of teams, players, results and the myriad details associated with a diverse range of sports, from hurling to boxing. On Sunday 29 September 2002, the final day of the Ryder Cup, Magee was chatting to Myles Dungan on RTÉ Radio in the course of previewing the twelve singles matches. Predictably, Magee put the days events in a historical context and recalled the feats of Eamonn Darcy, Christy Jr and Philip Walton and how each one had put an Irish stamp on the outcome.

Magee turned his attention to McGinley, who was scheduled to play in the ninth match of the afternoon. It was possible that it might prove to be a crucial match. Magee continued: 'You know I have a funny feeling…a premonition…that it will be Paul who will clinch victory for Europe…' Such an utterance would have been scoffed at had it come from any other commentator but a lifetime watching sporting events unfold had prompted this declaration. Magee wasn't indulging in wishful thinking, fortune-telling or a romantic fantasy. His instincts would prove to be spot-on.

LEAVING THE BIG BALL

Making the transition from Gaelic football to competitive golf was not without difficulties for McGinley.

I'm an ambitious guy and a naturally competitive person. Playing football during my youth influenced my team performances in golf. I love being part of a team and I missed that most about football.

It took me a few years when I turned professional to realise that, whilst the adrenalin in football and golf is the same, it has to be used in different ways. In football you push yourself and go into tackles hard. In golf the harder you try the less it happens. You cannot use your adrenalin in a physical sense at golf. You cannot muscle the ball around the course.

McGinley was a talented Gaelic football player, fearless to a fault, some might say. Golf was not his first sporting love. During his schooldays at Coláiste Éanna, Rathfarnham, football occupied his time. He continued to develop as a player with the Ballyboden St Enda's club. An injury forced him to take time out from football and he turned his attention to golf, primarily as a means of relaxation.

Until the age of nineteen, I was first and foremost a Gaelic footballer, playing at senior level. I got a bad injury – a broken kneecap in laymen's terms – and I was on crutches for nine months. They put a steel plate in my knee and I went through a huge amount of physiotherapy. When I finally got back on my feet, the doctor said, 'Look, there will be no more physical sports for you.' It was a massive blow because football was my first love. Golf took centre-stage after that.

His father, Michael, was the biggest early influence on his golf.

I learned a lot about the game and life in general from him. I used to caddy for him in the championships when I was younger. He instilled in me the ethics of the game, how to conduct myself, how to play the game and how to compete, also how to enjoy it. As an amateur golfer, after I quit football, I proceeded to make the Leinster team, then after a while I made the Irish team and after another while I played in the 1991 Walker Cup match at Portmarnock, which was a great thrill.

You can have all the talent in the world at eighteen

or nineteen or even your early twenties but there's no way you can appreciate the big picture. There are a few notable exceptions however, the most obvious being Tiger Woods. I was very raw when I turned professional. I was mature for my years, I knew about life and I was well travelled. Furthermore, I was educated and that helped me. But in terms of the golfing world I was raw and naïve.

I didn't exactly explode on to the golf scene as an amateur or as a professional. I was a slow learner and I wish things had come to me a lot quicker. Nothing I did was outstanding but, having said that, nothing I do is outstandingly bad. It took me a long time to find out what suited me best in terms of events and conditions.

McGinley was fortunate to have had excellent coaches throughout his career. His first coach was David Kinsella, the professional at Castle Golf Club.

David was the first person to actually teach me and to show me the correct techniques as a schoolboy. He gave me a very solid foundation. Then when I was about nineteen, I joined Grange and it was the great Watte Sullivan who helped me. His love of the game came through and he'd spend hours with the members on the practice ground, on the edge of the 18th, explaining technique and the mechanics of the swing.

When I was a member of the Irish amateur team there were John Garner and Howard Bennett. When I attended International University in San Diego my coach was Gordon Severson and I found the two years there very helpful. I walked on there and played my first year, never having been to America before. The level of competition there sharpened my game in all its aspects. I realised that I had moved from being a very raw amateur player to quite a decent level.

It was then that I felt that I had reached a stage that would enable me to make the transition to the pros. The year I left San Diego, I played in the Walker Cup and then turned pro. I tied for second at the European Tour school. That was the turning point for me. If I hadn't broken my kneecap, there would have been no way I'd have been a golfer. It wouldn't even have crossed my mind. I was gutted when I had to give up football but in retrospect, it was really a lucky break for me, literally.

Since turning professional I've been guided by Bob Torrance and Pete Cowen. After all these years I can tell you that the secret to golf is that there is no secret. There are no short-cuts. Golf is all about solid fundamentals. A good swing is based on strong fundamentals and understanding your swing and tendencies. The player I pay most attention to is Tom Watson, who has been my hero and role model since I was a kid. He stands for everything that's good about the game.

THE BELFRY 2002

In my whole career I've spent about 5 per cent of my time winning and I'm regarded as the most successful golfer ever to have played the game.

Jack Nicklaus to McGinley *circa* 1991

When McGinley played his way on to the 2002 Ryder Cup team he spoke about his expectations:

I'm really looking forward to it. I'm looking forward in a perverse way to experiencing the so-called scariness of the Ryder Cup. I'm told that the nerves are unbelievable. It will be interesting to discover how I deal with that at the Belfry.

In the days leading up to the matches he began to comprehend the magnitude of the occasion. 'I'm nervous and full of adrenalin,' he said. Such thoughts had not been helped by his recent dip in form.

> I was peaking last year but I'm not as good at the moment. But form always comes and goes in peaks and troughs. I have been busy working with my coach Pete Cowen and I feel that my game is improving.
>
> I will find out soon enough and it can't come soon enough. The best golf that's ever played anywhere always seems to be in the Ryder Cup. I don't know what it is about the intense atmosphere and the crowds but it always seems to bring out the best in players. You see more holes in one, chip-ins and long putts over those three days of competition than you do in three days anywhere else.

The teams were evenly matched in many ways, especially the mix of veterans and rookies. The US had three rookies, Europe four. There was considerable scrutiny of the form of the European players, whose games and ranking had slipped in the extra year. McGinley's play had dipped but he was optimistic that he would recover enough form to contribute in a meaningful way. 'I had some great players in the team,' Sam Torrance, the captain, said. 'All I had to do was point them in the right direction.'

McGinley was paired with Harrington in the afternoon foursomes and the Irish pair went down rather easily to Cink and Furyk 3 and 2. By the end of the first day's matches one point separated the teams. McGinley was paired with Clarke in the afternoon fourballs on day two. These match-ups were the closest of the week, with three games going to 18 and the fourth to 17. In the final match, McGinley and

Clarke struggled against Hoch and Furyk. They were 2-down after 14; McGinley then birdied 15 and 16 to tie the match. Hoch won the 17th to put the Americans in the lead.

As they made their way to the final hole, Sam Torrance was looking at another defeat. Then he had a brief meeting with Langer:

> Fritz made a great call as the final match of the second day went down the last, a significant one for us as the competition evolved. The match was all-square going down the 18th. With Darren furthest away after his tee shot found the right rough, Bernhard approached me.
>
> 'Sam,' he suggested. 'Why not get Paul to play first. There's less pressure on his shot and by playing before the other guys he could put some pressure on the Americans.' It seemed like a great idea so I wandered over to Paul and said, 'If you're okay with the prospect, we think maybe you should hit first.'
>
> He struck a wonderful 4-iron 200 yards to about twenty feet from the pin. Before getting ready to putt, Paul beckoned to me. 'Find Padraig and ask him if this was the putt we were talking about,' he whispered. Harrington was somewhere down the 18th fairway but we got confirmation relayed that it was indeed the putt. This was no trivial query; the putt swung more than one would expect and it was faster. Paul struck a lovely putt stone-dead. Both Americans bogeyed and McGinley's par tied the match 8-8. We were level going into the singles, for the first time since the 'War by the Shore' in 1991.
>
> More important, I felt, was the mood that winning the final hole established. To win the final hole of the day definitely raised our spirits. I liked Paul's game. He was very solid, a good putter and very tenacious. He was brilliant in the team-room, bubbly

and enthusiastic. I had played in enough Ryder Cups and knew enough Ryder Cup history to anticipate that some of the least likely players produce the most significant performances. McGinty would confirm this the following day.

From early on in the singles, victory never looked in doubt. At breakfast, Phillip Price, Pierre Fulke and McGinley spoke about the coming day's singles. 'One of us could be a hero today,' McGinley told the other two. And so it proved, with McGinley sinking the winning put in the process of tying with Jim Furyk.

McGinley played with distinction in the 2004 and 2006 matches. After the heroics of the Ryder Cup, he suffered through one of the worst slumps of his career. In addition he got tangled up in a confused situation with 2008 captain Nick Faldo, who had selected the Dubliner as a vice-captain for Valhalla. McGinley accepted the position with reluctance after Faldo put pressure on him.

It all came to a head during the Seve Trophy at the Heritage in September 2007. McGinley accepted that the source of the problems was him. 'It taught me that an active tournament golfer shouldn't attempt to wear two hats.' McGinley's tenure as vice-captain lasted four months.

How did this impact on his prospects for inclusion in the 2008 team? McGinley hoped to play his way on to the team.

I have nothing to say about the sequence of events, other than to express regret about the way the matter leaked out at the time. It's not what I would have wished in that it made me look bitter, which I wasn't.

I realised too late that I shouldn't have taken the job in the first place. There was confidential stuff which will remain that way. Like Nick's thoughts on players and other inside information. I certainly won't be giving Paul Azinger [US captain] an edge over a man I'm convinced is best equipped to keep the Ryder Cup this side of the Atlantic. He got my vote at the players' committee.

I regret the flak that Nick took from the media after the Seve Trophy but I thought he handled it very well…I knew that in all honesty, I couldn't stand eye to eye with Nick and give him an honest assessment of other players at a cost to myself. That's what happened at the Seve Trophy so it was time to clear the decks.

More than anybody that I've met in golf, Faldo is his own man. Single-mindedness is second nature to him, so he knew exactly where I was coming from. His parting words were to wish me the best in my attempt at qualifying for Valhalla. We haven't spoken since.

McGinley's comments on Faldo's role as captain are anything but superficial, based as they are on his experience of previous Cups.

The captain's record as a player really counts in the team-room. I remember the feeling at Oakland Hills [2004] when we could sit back and feel like the Manchester United players must feel, knowing that our man, Bernhard Langer, wasn't going to be outsmarted by Hal Sutton.

It was the same with Woosie at the K Club, where he was careful not to overdo the captain bit. Rather he let things flow, which is an art in itself. And I remember him telling us in our last team talk that we would all be playing on the opening day because he couldn't see any weakness. That's where Woosie was great. As for Faldo, you can take it he won't be outsmarted in Valhalla. He knows this game inside out. And he knows players. He can sense whether an individual is up for it. That's what he brings to the captain's table.

As the 2008 selection approached, McGinley was under no illusion about making a fourth successive Ryder Cup appearance.

> A lot of baloney has been talked about the composition of this year's team. People are getting way ahead of themselves. There's still a long way to go and the shape of the team will be determined by what happens during the next three months, not what has happened in the last nine, because a strong Ryder Cup team is about players in form.
>
> Like some of the other Irish lads, I've got to win, or finish second in a Major or another big money event. It's about massive money.

After thirty-six holes of this year's PGA at Wentworth, McGinley held a 4-shot lead and that vital win seemed likely, especially on his home course. A disastrous third-round 80 saw him fall back into the pack. He finished tenth but a glorious opportunity had passed him by. 'I was confident out there and playing well but it wasn't happening for me and a lot of putts didn't drop. Of course it was disappointing not to take advantage of a 4-shot lead.'

McGinley is a battler and his quest continues. 'I had the worst slump of my career last year but a new fitness regime is paying dividends. Quite simply, when I play well my head is good.'

After the frustrations of the previous eighteen months, making this year's Ryder Cup team would have been one of the most satisfying of McGinley's golfing achievements. He said, 'If I do get in, it will be with a clear mind. I would expect to have Faldo's respect for playing my way in and after all that's happened, that's something worth fighting for.'

It was not to be. McGinley found his form too late in the season. Rest assured, he will be keener than ever to be selected for the 2010 event.

14

PADDY HARRINGTON'S BOY

Sir Alex Ferguson turned to an unlikely source in his bid to push Manchester United to a repeat of last season's double heroics. Ferguson believed that his players could look at the example of Padraig Harrington retaining his Open golf title and winning the PGA Championship and at the capacity of Harrington and other top sportspeople to maintain their focus under extreme pressure. Ferguson was fulsome in his praise of Sunderland supporter Harrington and challenged his players to show similar drive and ambition in the months ahead: 'Harrington, under the severest of pressure, was so cool and showed me that he had the bottle. When he needed to perform in the last six holes, he had four birdies. He thoroughly deserved his victory.'

When he joined the European Tour in 1995, after three appearances in the Walker Cup, Padraig Harrington's ambitions were modest:

> My initial goal was to maintain my tour card, to finish around the middle of the pack in about seventieth spot at the end of year one. I had the idea that it would take a couple of years to get to the position where I felt comfortable and I just wanted to get in there and gain experience at the start before moving up.

His progress was more rapid than he had anticipated:

I expected that I'd have to cement my position and move on from that and in many ways that's what I've done. However, I came in a lot higher than expected at the start. Year one was unbelievably good and year two was even better.

The highlight of his first season was a victory in the Spanish Open, 16-under, 272 and a cheque for £91,660.

I really wanted to do well in my second season to prove that year one was no fluke. I felt I had to perform, as 1996 had been phenomenal, beyond my wildest dreams.

In 1997 one of the high points for him was a closing round of 67 in the British Open at Royal Troon for a share of fifth place. His brother Tadhg caddied for him in his early professional days as he had done during his amateur days. Tadhg was replaced by the legendary, colourful and experienced John O'Reilly.

As he prepared for the 1999 season, Harrington listed his goals on a personal computer:

I had three main goals – to make the Ryder Cup team, to improve my world ranking by making it into the top seventy-five and to win an event. I had five second-place finishes, which led to a lot of other good things. But you can only put up with that for so long. I don't know whether to cry or cheer about the sequence of second-place finishes. I need to start winning.

He made his début in the 1999 Ryder Cup at Brookline.

After his first win in Spain, he had a run of nine second-place finishes before he ended the drought in Brazil at the São Paolo 500 Years Open in early April 2000.

There are loads of things that I didn't achieve. By losing so many tournaments I know more about how to win. I've always felt that you've got to learn to win and I've always had to learn how to do things.

Sure, I should have won some of those tournaments but there were others where I had done well to be second. It certainly didn't bother me anyway, largely because of my amateur experience.

I was brought up with the amateur ethic and that concept of 'I don't mind failing, so long as I've tried my best' makes a lot of sense. So if I'm playing well, I know the rewards will come and the victories, too. Patience is an important virtue and I'm learning to take my time.

Harrington learned a valuable lesson at the Benson and Hedges International at the Belfry when it was discovered that he hadn't signed his card for Thursday's first round and he was disqualified when leading the field by five shots with just one round to play.

The first thing I did was tell my wife Caroline and then ring my mum, dad, brothers and everybody. I didn't want them to hear it from anyone else. And then I thought 'God, I'm ringing around as if there's been a death.'

So I didn't win the tournament. It's the same thing as if I teed up this week and didn't play very well. The great thing about being a professional golfer is that there's always next week. It's not a disaster. Nobody died. There is no one to blame but myself. We are professional golfers and, ultimately, we know that the responsibility for the card lies solely with ourselves.

The greatest piece of advice I've ever received came from my dad. When I was younger he told me that I shouldn't listen to well-meaning amateurs. I will listen to advice and take from it what I want but if I don't

like the advice, I just don't hear it. I recognise good
advice and I ignore bad advice.

Harrington's father was a Garda, a benevolent one. There are countless
stories of his giving taxi fares to drunks and giving youngsters a kick
up the backside and sending them on their way rather than arresting
them. He was a hard man but soft at the core.

> One of my earliest memories takes me back to Stackstown
> at four years of age. I was helping to level a green with my
> feet. I was lucky. My four older brothers had to pick up
> stones.

Paddy Harrington retired from the force at the age of fifty and
the father and youngest son spent many hours practising on the
range in Stackstown. Essentially they had twenty years together and
they became very close. 'My father never drank in the last thirty
years of his life. Maybe drink wasn't the best thing for him. But I'm
a teetotaller; I don't like the taste of alcohol. I never have. I couldn't
drink a whole beer.'

Harrington noticed a pronounced trend with alcohol dating back
to his amateur days.

> I saw right away that the players who drank – some
> of the most talented guys – did it to wash away
> expectations, as a kind of a built-in alibi. If they didn't
> win a match it was because of the six pints they had
> the night before. Maybe they didn't care for the stress
> and it was a way out really. I see a little of that in the
> pro game too.

Paddy Harrington was an accomplished inter-county footballer. He
played in two All Ireland finals with Cork, losing each time. He
boxed for the Gardaí and won a national title in his weight division.
Says Paul:

I'd still be known as Paddy Harrington's boy down in Cork. My father had absolutely no regrets about his Gaelic football career. I suppose he was content that in a team game he had given his all.

For a while I worried that I might have been the same, especially with all the runner-up positions, but then I began to understand the peace and content my father knew. That was very helpful to me in various ways through the ups and downs of my golf career.

It's worth noting that after Harrington Sr won his national boxing title he never boxed again. Try as he might he was unable to knock out his outclassed opponent, who suffered an almighty beating.

He won comfortably on points but he felt so bad about the hammering he gave this guy that he never boxed again. That tells you a lot about the man. That's the only trophy of his at home that I want to have some day.

Paul McGinley is one of Harrington's close friends. They attended the same school, Coláiste Éanna in Rathfarnham. Paul says:

I knew Padraig first as a Gaelic footballer, a goalkeeper. I was fourteen and I think he was about eleven and we lived within a mile of each other. We were friendly enough at that point but not close. That side developed after we paired to win the World Cup in 1997. I know his mother. I knew his father well. Lovely man. Great footballer. My own father used to talk about him.

Padraig is the youngest in the family, with four brothers – Tadhg, Columb, Fintan and Fergal. The older boys spoiled him when they began earning money. But he knows his place in the pecking order; the brothers cheerfully remind him of that. He may be a superstar in the golf world but he's just an ordinary guy around the family.

That's the way he wants it and in any case the brothers wouldn't have it any other way. They are all equally proud of one another's accomplishments.

Harrington developed his skills on the tricky, winding Stackstown course. With its tight 100 acres, the premium was on getting the ball on the ground as quickly as possible and driving it straight. Consequently he was an outstanding chipper and putter, who tended to be short and straight. He was never regarded as pro material even after an outstanding amateur career. His swing would need serious attention. Darren Clarke remembers those days:

> Golf always came relatively easily to me. I never had to work as hard as Padraig. He showed up with a great short game and a not so great full swing. To be honest he didn't look the part but then he'd frustrate the hell out of you. I was a few years ahead of him but I knew he'd go after me. He was never intimidated then or now. I turned pro just in time!

Harrington was reluctant to join the professional ranks:

> I turned pro basically because all the guys I was beating were turning pro. I didn't expect to be a star in the game of golf. I was never destined to be a star. Everybody said I didn't have the swing for it. I never played in a pro-event as an amateur. That should tell you something.

BOB TORRANCE, SWING COACH, AGED SEVENTY-SIX
Harrington has his own room in the Torrance home, the Ben Hogan suite. He is the only golfer to be given this accommodation. Torrance is a feisty, crusty heart-of-gold type of man. There are many similarities between Bob and his only son, Sam, except for the teary eyes the son is prone to. Bob is a chain-smoking coffee-drinking guy, eminently quotable, a devotee of Ben Hogan but also an admirer of the legendary Harvey Penick:

Harvey's teachings were simple. They should be. Golf's hard enough. At the same time if you learn something too quickly in golf, you'll lose it too early. Padraig came to me after I had worked with Paul McGinley for a few years and the only thing of Padraig's that I never changed was his grip. His leg action was especially bad. You might have noticed, it's better.

Torrance is a teacher in the old-fashioned mould, no gimmicks, no video cameras or fancy technology. He watches and can see the deficiencies quite quickly. Then he'll 'show you something,' and that leads to another thing and so the teaching and learning takes place. When he knows that the golfer understands what he is trying to achieve he'll smile.

BROOKLINE, 1999

'America will win the Ryder Cup next month,' George Peper, former editor of *Golf Magazine*, told this writer, 'if only for the reason that when you look at the European team, you wonder who the hell are half these guys. We can't even get their names right.' He paused briefly, waited a moment and sighed. 'But we've been saying that since the mid-1980s and we keep getting our asses kicked.'

Ernie Els, Nick Price and others had been hinting that the Europeans 'might be blown out of the water'. David Feherty knew better: 'On paper this is a very formidable American team but they would want to concentrate on beating someone they've never heard of before. If they don't they're liable to get beaten again at Brookline.'

Padraig became one of those no-name rookies when he finished second in the BMW tournament in Munich. He left it late; two weeks before he was a distant sixteenth in the Ryder Cup standings.

The whole way through the Ryder Cup campaign all I had to do was win a tournament. Okay, I didn't quite win one but two second places is as good as one win. I knew what I had to do and the hype wasn't on me.

His performances won him an invitation to the WGC NEC Invitational in Akron, Ohio, a pleasant and lucrative reward for Padraig and his wife Caroline.

> Once you make the team, that battle is over. You're on to a new one. There's no point in being happy about making the team. I have to play well when I get there. I don't want to play on a losing team and I don't want to play badly.
>
> One thing that I've learned from all the teams I've played on through my career, is that after making a team you tend to forget about that and concentrate on performing when you have to.

Harrington would maintain that approach through all his subsequent Ryder Cup campaign

He was not lacking in confidence approaching the Ryder Cup format. 'Matchplay certainly brought the best out me as an amateur, so I am going to try and resurrect that kind of attitude that I had back in those days. Four years down the line as a pro, I've probably forgotten a lot of my matchplay tendencies.' Those tendencies never faded, not in a player who defeated Tiger Woods in the 1995 Walker Cup.

> It was myself and Jody Flanagan. We won handily enough, 3 and 2 or something like that. And as far as the Ryder Cup goes I'm not concerned about who my opponent is. I'd only tend to be worried about myself and that's it. I have enough to do trying to get my game in shape. I'm sure my opponents can look after themselves.

The role of underdog appealed to him:

That's going to help us without a doubt. They [the Americans] are under pressure to do well and they're the favourites. We have seven rookies in the team, which is going to help us in that we're all in the same boat. We can help each other out and certainly feel for what the others are going through. There will be a great bond between the rookies in the team.

Back in Dublin, 'reaction is massive, overwhelming and they're all delighted of course'. None more so than Paddy Harrington.

He's both happy and relieved. He was looking at the downside of it: if I had kept on dropping shots he was worried that it would damage my confidence for the rest of my career. But it wouldn't have bothered me if I didn't make the team again. What would have bothered me seriously would be to have five shots of a lead and lose it. Yeah, I'd say my dad was very relieved all right!

Making the Ryder Cup team was a milestone in Harrington's career and his father savoured the magnitude of the achievement.

My dad never put any pressure on me to play well. He's always supported me. He says he's already lived his sporting career and doesn't need to live a second one through me. He has his own athletic identity. That terrific family support has always been very helpful but never overbearing.

Harrington cringes when he sees parents who are being too pushy with their kids and sport:

I hate to see it. I'd be fearful of that carry-on, especially if a youngster is pushed so far that the fun goes out of it. That was what was so special about my dad when I started

to concentrate on golf. We had great times together, a lot
of laughter. I feel very fortunate in that respect.

Harrington experienced the inevitable nerves common to all first-
time Ryder Cup players. 'I'd heard plenty of stories about Ryder Cup
débuts and, naturally, I will never forget my first match in the Ryder
Cup.' He was paired with Miguel-Angel Jimenez, who was in superb
form at that time. They faced the formidable Americans, Davis Love
and Payne Stewart. 'Miguel left me with a 7-iron to the green but I
was so nervous I could hardly see the ball. I seemed to be standing
over the ball for ages.' They went on to halve the match and the
worst of Harrington's nerves subsided.

Harrington went out to play Mark O'Meara in the singles. The
Americans started the final-day singles with a flourish and won 7
points to bring them back into serious contention. They won their
matches with conviction. A win for O'Meara against Harrington
would likely turn over the Europeans. The crowds began to grow as
the match headed into the back 9 all-square.

Harrington was aware of the points situation. The exhortations
of the American fans made that very clear. The match turned on the
16th hole.

> Mark James was waiting for me on the sixteenth and one
> look at him told me all I needed to know. Fortunately, I hit
> a terrific shot into that green. Under the circumstances,
> the noise, the atmosphere and my level of excitement, it
> has to be one of my best ever shots. O'Meara's ball found
> a bunker and he made bogey to put me 1-up, which I
> held.

Harrington secured the first European point of the day on the 18th
hole and what he believed was the winning putt in the Ryder Cup.
His excitement was short-lived, thanks to Justin Leonard's heroics
on the 17th hole.

Harrington was disappointed that Europe lost but not to the

point of devastation, as were many of his team-mates. He coped well with the defeat.

> I wasn't especially bothered by what happened near the end. It says a lot for European golf that the Americans reacted the way they did. It showed how much winning the Ryder Cup meant to them and you have to credit them for that amazing comeback.

Harrington was singled out for alleged slow play in his match against O'Meara, especially by the NBC commentators. Indeed, the same commentators weren't too kind to the US team. One would have expected more understanding from these seasoned observers: they failed to grasp the magnitude of Harrington's shot on the 17th as he paced the yardage. Harrington retains an ambivalent attitude to the 1999 Ryder Cup:

> It was certainly an experience but I'm not sure I'd call it a good one. On reflection you say it was great and you remember all the positive features. And you say I want to do it again, I want to have that experience again but not because it was enjoyable. Unlike going to a film, the Ryder Cup is a lived experience and it stays with you forever.

THE BELFRY 2002

Harrington got off to a disappointing start at the Belfry, losing his first two matches, in which he was paired with Niclas Fasth and Paul McGinley. In truth he was playing poorly and he wasn't afraid to let Sam Torrance know about it.

He asked to be paired with Colin Montgomerie, who was playing very well, and the strategy worked. They beat Phil Mickelson and David Toms by 2 and 1 and Harrington had his first point. This would pave the way for what he regards as one of his best ever performances against Mark Calcavecchia in the singles.

Harrington used the fear factor to good effect. He didn't want to be blown away by Calcy, who was a streaky performer. However, when he was on his game he was capable of overwhelming any player. Harrington is often at his best when he plays in fear. His focus is enhanced and his frame of mind is exactly where he wants it to be in tight situations. He knew there would be pressurised situations against the American and he found himself in the thick of one at the 8th hole.

Harrington hit a horrible tee shot that ended up in the water. The 8th hole was difficult that day, playing into the wind. It opened the door for the American, who played down the right hand side of the fairway to avoid going in the water. It was a sensible shot but crucially for Harrington, it didn't find the fairway. Harrington took a penalty drop and his wood shot found a greenside bunker.

Calcavecchia didn't find the green from his lie, chipped up and missed the putt. Harrington got up and down from the sand for a half. Effectively the match was over.

> That broke his heart. He was 2-down at that stage. When you can't win a hole after the kind of shot I played on the 8th you start to feel that there's no way of beating this guy.

Harrington never gave him an opportunity of getting back into the match. He knew the dangers of letting up, of losing the fear. He won by 5 and 4. Harrington was one of the earlier finishers that day and he watched the other matches. 'The best part was watching Paul hole the winning putt on the final green. Under the circumstances, it was a huge moment the way Paul finished it off, tremendously exciting.'

OAKLAND HILLS 2004

Harrington started this match in dreamlike fashion. He was paired with Monty for the opening match against Phil Mickelson and Tiger Woods and they won the opening hole and never looked back. This victory set the tone for the entire tournament. The Europeans had beaten the so-called 'dream team' by 2 and 1. 'We weren't given much hope against them but that gave us all the motivation we needed. And we were well up for the challenge.'

In the afternoon foursomes, Harrington teamed up with McGinley against Tiger and Davis Love. Harrington started poorly and the Irish pairing were 2-down early. 'I wasn't up for it,' he would say later.

> Paul saw this and pulled me aside. He bailed me out big time at that point. Thankfully, I began to get into the flow of the match and started to make a few shots.
>
> After we finally took the lead it was fairly easy. Who would have believed that beforehand? Of course there was a huge Irish contingent following this match and to win it on the 15th green was a great Irish occasion. It was massive to beat Tiger and Davis by 4 and 3. They could do little right once they fell behind.

With a lead of 11-5 going into the singles, nobody on the European team was taking anything for granted. Harrington was the last out on the final day against veteran Jay Haas. By the time they reached the 14th hole the outcome had been decided.

Harrington managed to prevail over Haas on the 18th hole, meaning that he had won all his singles matches in the Ryder Cup to that point. It was difficult for Harrington because the pressure was off. 'I don't agree with playing out when the overall result has been decided. I think it should be called a half and off you go.' The Americans were beaten by a total of nine points on their own soil.

PLAYING WITH FEAR

'Experience is a hard teacher because she gives the test first, the lesson afterwards.' That well-worn adage was central to the mindset of Padraig Harrington as he began the 2004 season. 'I've never wanted to play golf as much since turning pro. To be honest I'm fed up with practice. It's time to take the show on the road.'

The sign of a great athlete is that he has a high tolerance for failure and learns to view it as feedback. Few golfers exemplify this more than Harrington. The Irishman is a bewildering, perplexing player. There's a perception that he has failed to deliver when it counts (for instance, late in the day in the Open at Muirfield in 2002), that he is too intense, falling victim to psych-outs and traps. He has suffered from a uniquely Irish form of disparagement. When he is successful the nation goes hysterical but a perceived failure is met with criticism. Again, this 2004 season, Harrington would be judged by what he does not achieve.

> I've worked on all elements of my swing for a number of years and now it's just a question of putting them together and keeping it going. My schedule is there to suit my game, not my pocket. I'm not going to change that, especially since the birth of my son Patrick. Eventually, I do want to play more in the States. I took a lot of confidence from 2003. There was a question at the end of 2002 as to whether I peaked and got the most out of my game. There's definitely more in the tank.
>
> Last year showed I can be in the top ten while playing average. I know now how to improve and the thing is to bring the improvement to the course when I get out there. Probably the next ten years will see me peak age-wise. I'm ready to play golf now and I think I'm through the phase of building a golf swing. Now I want to build a competitive game.

It's rare for a modern athlete to admit self-doubt and fear. Not so Harrington:

> After my winter break every year, I'll be wondering when I come back out if it's still there. I think everybody does. I play with fear, which may sound odd

but it keeps my mind on the task. I've never had much success with confidence. It makes me vulnerable to being a bit cocky within myself and mistakes happen.

Winning a Major is the ultimate goal. I hope that one day I'll be in contention in a Major and do the right thing. I probably let one get away [Muirfield 2002] and I regret that certainly.

Armed with hindsight, the critics questioned his shot-making when it was his normally reliable putting that let him down. 'I played great golf for seventy-two holes and ironically my strongest point became my weakest link. However, that showed me I had a game besides just chipping and putting.'

So much for the critics.

Bob Torrance reiterated a long-held belief in his pupil: 'Nobody works harder than Padraig. He has everything it takes to win a big one and if he gets another chance he'll take it.'

Harrington added:

I'm certainly capable of winning a Major but it's not something I expect to happen as a matter of course. If I play my best golf, I'll give myself a chance sooner or later. I'd be quietly confident anyway. I don't mind failing if I let it all out there.

In that Ryder Cup year – 2004 – Harrington's attitude revealed a harder edge to his make-up.

The Ryder Cup is an interesting event and it's a lot of pain to go through. You're trying to make a team to go through what's one of the toughest experiences of your life when you get there. If you make the team early you can anticipate the event and enjoy it a bit more. But it's hard going in August if you're fighting for every point.

Harrington's perceived failures, give-aways and chokes were forgotten when he bridged the Major gap in Irish golf.

THE K CLUB 2006

It was another comprehensive victory for the Europeans and reflected well on the sporting, enthusiastic Irish golf fans. Harrington was not at his best but after the long lead-in to the Cup and the hype surrounding it, he was relieved that the event was memorable for all the right reasons. He may have been mentally drained because of being the poster boy for the event.

Harrington has been an advocate of mental fitness since his amateur days when he began working with psychologist Aidan Moran in Dublin. When he joined the pro ranks he sought the help of the Belgian, Jos Vanstiphout. It's ironic that Harrington plays his best golf when he is afraid, yet he employs the services of mental coaches to offset certain fears. This is not a negative observation because Harrington is so thorough in his preparation that he will take on board anything that helps to improve his performance.

Bob Rotella is Harrington's mental coach and author of several books on the mental side of the game. He is regarded as being perhaps the best at what he does. '95 per cent of the game is mental,' Harrington says, 'and I'm trying to become the best golfer I can be.'

Rotella stayed with him at the Torrances' house and was on hand when Harrington won the 2007 British Open. One can't help asking if Harrington needs the input of a mental coach. He is a well-rounded individual, always certain of the unstinting support of parents, siblings, wife and children.

His response is that the ordinary punter, sports writer, golf fan, can never truly know what a player is thinking in specific situations. 'They are making judgments without all the information. They don't know what is going on inside a player's head. And this applies to Tiger, the world's best player and to all professionals.' This is a characteristic, reasoned Harrington comment.

OPEN CHAMPION 2007 – BREAKING THE BARRIER

Harrington answered all the questions and quieted his critics by winning the British Open in 2007, the first Irishman from the twenty-six counties to bring the Claret Jug home. This will be remembered as one of the finest moments in Irish sport and a highlight of Harrington's career. It was a defining accomplishment for Harrington and for Irish professional golfers in general. He repeated the achievement in 2008.

Des Smyth understands the implications of this better than most:

> I've been saying for years that we have the talent in Ireland to play with the best in the world. It's baffling that we had to wait so long for Padraig to do it, when you think of how close Christy Sr came, only to be denied – and not just once. Darren came close as well. Padraig's win is important because he has broken through the barrier. He has won a Major. The other Irish lads will take heart from that and be inspired to emulate it. This is especially so because Padraig never stood out at any point as a likely winner. When I first saw him play my impression was a great short game, problematic swing but a hard worker.
>
> His win is a testament to hard work, perseverance and commitment. He always loved having a go against players who were ranked higher. What a player to have in your side. He has given it everything to this point and you'd expect him to win. I think it's great that young Irish golfers look up to him and marvel at his achievements.

As expected, Padraig Harrington made the 2008 Ryder Cup team without any difficulty, this time as a double Major-winner.

15

The Man Who Brought
the Ryder Cup to Ireland

Ireland's tradition of links golf is well documented. It's a huge selling point for golfing visitors, especially Americans. When the prospect of hosting the Ryder Cup in Ireland came up for discussion, there was a tacit understanding that a links venue would prevail in the selection process.

According to the traditionalist or purist viewpoint, links golf represented the spiritual home of Irish golf. The idea of playing it elsewhere was viewed as a betrayal of traditional values, a sellout of the soul of Irish golf.

Michael Smurfit had other ideas. The wealthy businessman also had the vision and financial wherewithal to implement them. His pursuit of the Ryder Cup began in the summer of 1998. He said:

> The first objective was to get it for Ireland and we had formal confirmation of that in Valderrama last September [1997]. Now the key question is location and all that that entails. With regard to here [the K Club] we have certain things which we need to do if we are to stage the Ryder Cup. And in that context five or six years is a very short time [the 9/11 attacks would put the event back a year].
>
> For example we will need planning permission for an extension to the hotel and that's two years, maybe more. Then there is the building programme, another

year or two. That's the bulk of the time gone. From our perspective, we need to know certainly no later than the middle of next year [1999], preferably earlier.

The announcement was made in January 1999.

There is the merchandising of the event. Ryder Cup Ireland has a magical ring to it. It's going to be huge for this country.

Smurfit was in no doubt that the K Club had earned the right to stage the event.

I think it's important to note that we've been sponsoring junior golf in Ireland for a long period of time. Before any talk of the Ryder Cup came up, I don't think people could have doubted our commitment to the game. There was the sponsorship of the Irish Professional Championship, the Christy O'Connor Pro-Am and the European Open. But we were always aware of competition out there.

Smurfit was very mindful of the argument that a links course would be a more appropriate venue. His response was pragmatic and pointed:

That's what we used to sell but golfing in Ireland is no longer just about links courses. The whole scene has been changed by the development of top-quality parkland courses. For instance, our course is booked out for a considerable length of time. You may argue that we limit the number of rounds played here but at our prices per round, the income is as good as 50,000 rounds elsewhere. I would suggest that we've proved the demand is there if the quality is right.

Our main rivals for the Ryder Cup are Portmarnock

and Mount Juliet. I would be very disappointed if we're not favourites going in but that's not to suggest for one moment that we're complacent. I acknowledge and respect the traditionalist view. Mount Juliet has strong credentials.

We've had a number of Americans over, such as Tiger Woods, Mark O'Meara, Payne Stewart and Tom Lehman [the 2006 US captain]. And we asked their genuine opinion. Most of them don't know Portmarnock although I gather O'Meara played there in the 1987 Irish Open. The response has been very encouraging.

Smurfit concluded: 'The Americans would favour a course like this, which might not necessarily help our bid, from a competitive standpoint. But that's for the Ryder Cup committee to decide.' The decision was favourable to Smurfit and the K Club was selected. As the 2006 matches approached, the 'North Course' was renamed the 'Palmer Course.' Arnold Palmer was a very visible presence during the week of the Ryder Cup. Michael Smurfit could feel vindicated.

16

The K Club 2006

After what seemed an interminable wait, the Ryder Cup finally got under way in County Kildare, a year later than originally scheduled. There was a protracted lead-in to the matches and the visual impact of the Ryder Cup logo was in evidence all over the country, from buses, bus stops, health foods and sporting drinks to T-shirts and golf shirts. The advertising campaign was quite effective and Ryder Cup tickets became much sought-after items.

Padraig Harrington was the poster boy for the Irish Ryder Cup. For a period there was a possibility that Harrington would not play his way on to the team. This would have been problematic for captain Ian Woosnam: Harrington was always going to participate in the matches but Woosnam was hoping not to have to give up a precious wildcard pick to ensure this.

Harrington took part in the French Open, a tournament he had not hitherto fitted into his schedule. However, with a hefty amount of Ryder Cup points available, Harrington finished in second place, clinching his spot. Paul McGinley worked incessantly and once again qualified for the team. When Woosnam offered Darren Clarke a wildcard pick, the Big Three were there for the third successive Ryder Cup.

With Des Smyth as one of Woosnam's vice-captains, it could hardly have been better. Although an Irishman was not selected as captain, in Des Smyth the Europeans got considerably more than the next best thing. Says Feherty: 'I think the Europeans got the trump card when Smythy came on board. His presence, maturity and his desire to win were intangibles the Americans did not have.

Effectively, Europe had two captains and Smythy's role should not be underestimated. It was anything but a ceremonial one.'

There was a palpable sense of relief and satisfaction in Harrington's comment at the time:

> You don't like to make too much of these things in public but I'm very proud for myself and for my family that I'm playing in the Ryder Cup for the fourth successive match. I know Paul and Darren feel very much the same way and it certainly is great for Ireland to have three of our players in the side for the third successive match.
>
> I hope the weather brightens up and the fans can enjoy themselves. And hopefully we can play our part by giving them something to cheer.

With the exception of the weather Harrington got his wish. The rains came, accompanied by severe winds, and lingered for much of the tournament.

The Irish fans turned up anyway. They had waited a long time for this historic event and weather conditions would not deter them. Over 40,000 (predominantly Irish) men and women of all ages turned out on each of the practice days and for the match itself. The more affluent Celtic Tigers arrived by helicopter – six hundred drops a day for the duration of the competition.

It was apparent from the opening morning of play that the Americans were going to be up against it. Tiger Woods hooked his opening drive into the lake as Darren Clarke split the fairway and birdied the first hole. That laid down a marker for the rest of the matches. A trend was established that was never reversed and the anticipated close contest never materialised.

Europe entered the final day leading 10-6, needing only four points from the twelve singles to retain the trophy, plus another half-point to win again for the fourth time in five matches. It was then that the home supporters came into their own. If the Europeans needed a lift, they got it from the moment they stepped on to the first tee. The Americans were also well received and generously applauded as they entered the playing area.

The place erupted when the Europeans made their entrance to each match. There was a football-like atmosphere, singing and serenading and sustained ear-splitting cheers and applause. Garcia and Olazabal were given the customary 'Olé! Olé! Olé!' welcome, while Harrington and MiGinley were treated to a rousing rendition of 'Molly Malone'.

Montgomerie was given a reception the likes of which he had never experienced; he was moved. He saluted the fans by raising his hand and gave them a distinctive shake of the head. Monty was among his own; these were the fans who understood and appreciated him and his contribution over the years. It was one of many memorable moments on that final day.

When Darren Clarke entered the area of the first tee, everyone in the stands rose to give him a prolonged ovation. His opponent, Zach Johnson had anticipated what the crowd's reaction to Clarke might be – or so he thought. 'I expected it to be loud,' he said, 'but it was like a football-stadium crowd of 80,000 massed around one tee box. It was pretty remarkable. I felt like I was the away team, playing for the world championship, or something, in another sport.'

American captain Tom Lehman knew it was imperative to get points on the board early if his team was to reverse the deficit. He sent out his top players – David Toms, Stewart Cink, Jim Furyk and Tiger Woods – in the hope of putting four points on the board.

He placed his four rookies in the middle and slotted Phil Mickelson, Chris DiMarco and Scott Verplank at the bottom end. His thinking was sound and on paper it was hard to quibble with his decision. The success of this strategy was wholly dependent on the Americans winning early and often. Stewart Cink, one of the PGA Tour's finest putters, did his part for the Americans by trouncing Garcia, even though the Spaniard had played well. Cink rained in putts from all distances and was unbeatable. This match finished early on the 15th hole.

Tiger defeated the Swede, Robert Karlsson, 3 and 2 despite losing his 9-iron to the Liffey in bizarre circumstances on the 7th hole. Watched by his friend Michael Jordan, Woods was unfazed and by the time his putter was recovered from the river the match was finished. The Americans had two points on the board but thereafter Lehman's strategy crumbled.

Montgomerie gained the first European point on Sunday. He had to take the tenacious David Toms to the 18th hole to win but he was never in any real danger. Paul Casey made it 12-8 when he closed out Furyk on the 17th green.

David Howell made it 13-8 for Europe by defeating Brett Wetterich 5 and 2.

When Luke Donald beat Chad Campbell, Europe was guaranteed at least a draw and retention of the trophy. The Americans were down and all but finished. There was an inevitability about the outcome now and all that remained to be seen was who would make the winning putt. That distinction fell to Sweden's Henrik Stenson, when he defeated Vaughn Taylor 4 and 3. The score of 15-8 guaranteed a European victory and roars of approval were heard throughout the course. Because of simultaneous cheers from around the course Stenson didn't know that his putt was to win the Cup.

Darren Clarke had been positioned in the seventh singles against Zach Johnson. Woosnam gambled that Clarke's match might be the one to secure the winning point. It was a prescient strategy by Woosnam and it almost came off. With the Cup won, all eyes turned to Clarke's match with Johnson.

Both players made their way up the 16th fairway, having played their approach shots to the green. Clarke was 3-up at that point.

The ropes came down and the spectators spilled on to the fairway and crossed toward the river bank for the closest possible vantage point. Clarke duly finished off Johnson and what happened next will long be talked about. The roars erupted and Clarke was approached by players from both teams. One by one they came to him and hugged him.

Zach Johnson summed it up best:

I think as a player we all know what he can do and how good he really is. But he's an even better person...it was a lot of emotion, obviously more for him than me. And, I don't know, I could have had my A-plus game and I'm not sure I could have beat him. The gods were on his side. He's a great guy.

It was six weeks to the day since Darren Clarke's wife, Heather, had died.

Europe had won the Ryder Cup but there was unfinished business out on the course. Ian Woosnam was hoping that the winning margin might be extended. 'This is important to the guys who are playing,' says Des Smyth. 'It's a team game and you want to win as many matches as possible so there's no letdown even after the Cup is won.'

Paul McGinley was playing the 17th hole, in the match ahead of Clarke. The massive roar from behind the 16th green told him that Clarke had won. McGinley and J.J. Henry were all-square in a very tight match. After the turn they matched par for par until they arrived at the 17th hole. McGinley's third shot assured him of a tap-in birdie, while Henry faced a difficult breaking thirty-footer to keep the match alive.

While Henry was preparing to take his putt, a male streaker emerged from behind the ropes and made his way to the edge of the green. McGinley told the intruder to disappear and approached Des Smyth for advice. 'He was fairly intent on conceding the 30-foot putt,' said the vice-captain, 'and I told him the decision was his own, it was his call to make.' McGinley walked down to Henry and conceded the putt to halve the match. It was a magnanimous gesture by the Dubliner.

'I felt it was the right thing to do,' he said. 'There were those who felt the streaker should have been pushed into the lake and told to go swimming for Tiger's 9-iron.'

Henry appreciated the gesture:

I think it shows what the spirit of this competition is all about, what a gentleman Paul is…We did have some extra-curricular activities going on at the same time. We had a great match, neck-and-neck virtually the entire way. I tip my hat to him: it was a remarkable thing he did.

As he walked off the 18th green, McGinley's thoughts turned to Clarke.

'Did Darren hole the winning putt?' he asked. But there was no disappointment when he was told that Stenson had. The consummate team member, McGinley was delighted for the Swede but even more so for the team.

'Nobody understands how good this team is and how good our European Tour is. For the last two years, I've been saying our European Tour is going to make this the toughest team ever to make, because the standard is so good, the scoring is so good.' Two years on and the talent on the European Tour was even deeper, as Des Smyth pointed out.

It was a defining moment for McGinley, who understood better than most the magnitude of the achievement:

I'm so, so proud. I'm very emotional. I'm proud not just for me and the team but for the Irish people and the way they behaved this week, bar that clown on the last green. I'm just very, very proud. We put on a great show. All credit to Dr Smurfit and the Irish Tourism Board, but most obviously the team.

Meanwhile, Harrington was still battling with Scott Verplank in the last singles match. It wasn't a particularly auspicious Cup for Harrington. He played well but came up against an opponent who had something to prove. Verplank, a captain's pick, had played in only one match (a win) before the singles.

American television analyst, Johnny Miller, described Verplank in the previous day's fourballs as 'dead wood'. Verplank heard the comments in the American dressing room. Miller, a former Major winner, is a knowledgeable golf analyst. He is known for his blunt commentary but he comes across as arrogant and none too subtle. David Feherty he is not.

It was an inappropriate comment and Harrington felt the backlash from a highly motivated Verplank. The highlight of this skilfully-played contest came on the 213 yard par-3 14th hole, when Verplank scored a hole in one, the sixth in Ryder Cup history. This left the American 4-up with four to play and he closed out the match on the 15th hole.

It was a personal triumph for Verplank and vindicated his selection. Two matches, two wins muted the criticism expressed by Miller. On another day, Harrington might have won. Verplank had four birdies and an eagle while Harrington had three birdies. Europe's winning margin was 18½ to 9½, identical to their margin of two years previously.

Darren Clarke's summing up said it best:

> Woosie has been great. I can't remember an occasion where we've had twelve players playing so well. His only dilemma was who to rest and who to play. You can see from the result that he chose wisely. He's been a great captain. He's done absolutely everything perfectly. And, I think, the bottom line is that the score reflected this. It's pretty huge to follow up that result from Detroit a couple of years ago and to do it again.

The disappointed Americans accepted their defeat graciously. There could be no excuses, so comprehensive was the defeat. There was the inevitable criticism and second-guessing and questioning of the team's resolve. 'Our team gave it all that we had,' said Tom Lehman. 'We wanted to give it our very best effort, to play with heart, to have courage…but I guess the Europeans just played better. They played great golf, made a lot of putts. They played a phenomenal golf tournament.'

Tiger Woods was the leading points-scorer on the US team. It was scant consolation. 'Losing doesn't sit well, nor should it. We went out there, we played and they just outplayed us. They made more putts than we did.'

Jim Furyk gave perhaps the most thorough and considered response:

> Everyone wants answers. I don't think there is a guy who can give the answer on what is different. I think it's actually a good time for reflection. You can run with it probably a million different ways...we've obviously been outplayed in all aspects and we've just done a horrendous job in the five Ryder Cups I've played in. In four of them we did a horrendous job on Friday and Saturday in team play. I guess if we had all the answers and they were that simple, the results would probably be a little bit better for us.

For Des Smyth, there was a simpler explanation. 'This is possibly the best team Europe has ever assembled. They're one heck of a good team and quite a few of them will be around for a while.'

17

THE NEXT GENERATION:
McDOWELL, McGRANE, McILROY

GRAEME MCDOWELL

> This kid can be the best Irish golfer of all time. While
> I expect Harrington to win a Major, McDowell has
> God-given talent. He has what I call the 'ability to win
> gene'.
>
> Butch Harmon

This was heady praise for the young Portrush native. Butch Harmon, former coach to Tiger Woods, Greg Norman, Fred Couples and several high-profile professionals, is not a man given to hyperbole. After a lifetime playing and coaching in golf he is forthright with his comments and commands respect on both sides of the Atlantic. Harmon's prediction about Harrington's Major win has been vindicated. McDowell is now beginning to deliver on his vast potential and the heavy weight of expectation that accompanies it. Harmon pointed to a more immediate asset:

> He knows his strengths and he has been a prolific winner
> at every level. Mentally he is very strong, yet relaxed. He
> is very intelligent and doesn't obsess about the game.
> Having said that, he needs to start bringing it home on
> Sunday. Potential is just another word for having won
> nothing and he is well aware of that.

McDowell didn't make the 2006 Ryder Cup. Because of his early success in the professional ranks, there was a presumption that selection on the Ryder Cup team was inevitable. It was not to be: McDowell didn't play his way on to the team as expected and his role was confined to the television studio. His discomfiture in the commentary booth had nothing to do with on-air nerves. He is very comfortable in the media spotlight and is quick minded and witty.

Although he was reluctant to acknowledge his disappointment at not making the 2006 team, it was a setback for him.

> I should have been on that team and not in the commentary booth. It didn't happen for a number of reasons but essentially I didn't play well enough to be out there. Yes, of course, it hurt not to be a part of that historic occasion but I will do everything possible to ensure that I qualify for the next [2008] matches.

Events proved him right for 2008.

McDowell's professional career got off to the best possible start when he won the Scandinavian Open in 2002, on just his fourth appearance on the European Tour.

> I was very pleased it all happened so quickly. It took the pressure off so I was able to relax and play my own game. I didn't have to worry about making enough money to get my card.
>
> On the other hand, when I won in Scandinavia I was coming off the back of some really good amateur golf. I got in the lead and didn't really know what else to do but go ahead and win. In retrospect, everything just happened too fast and I didn't know how to react to the win. I didn't truly feel like a professional. My mindset was very much that of a competitive amateur.
>
> That early win took the pressure off and I was at a loose end. Consequently, I didn't have a breaking-in

period. My work ethic dropped off and I didn't know where to go from there. I played much of the 2003 season in a bit of a daze and I was totally lacking a support network when my game began to falter.

At the Tavistock Cup, in April 2008, a different personality beamed from the television screens live from Isleworth Country Club in Florida and McDowell was seen chatting easily and amicably with Tiger Woods. McDowell had arrived in America; hence the invitation to play in the members-only Tavistock Cup. The Ulsterman is comfortable fraternising with the top players even though he failed to retain his PGA Tour card in 2006.

The implications of this sense of belonging were not lost on David Feherty:

Aye, Tiger is comfortable with Graeme. It has to be that Ulster thing again, you know: the young man is gregarious, personable and relaxed. His smile is genuine and warm, unlike the contrived grins that some players put on for the cameras. Tiger has taken all this on board. He knows the genuine article and they get along fine. Graeme is very articulate and a very serious golfer. The nice thing about him is he doesn't take himself too seriously.

After an outstanding amateur career McDowell took his game to another level when he attended the University of Alabama. There he came under the influence of Alan Kaufman:

When he came over here he was just an average player. He didn't hit the ball long but he hit it very straight. In three years he went from a short hitter who hit it straight to a long hitter who hit it straight, and he went from a very mediocre putter to a very good putter. His personality and his intelligence were the key to his progression here. Obviously he worked at the fundamentals but they all do.

Kaufman was equally optimistic about McDowell's future in the professional game:

> Look, he's not in the Tiger Woods category at all but then who is? He is certainly in the Paul Casey, Adam Scott, Luke Donald category. They are all excellent players. Is he gonna be the next great Irish player? That's a question I don't dwell on but there's no reason why he won't. He ain't proved it yet, however.

It cam as no surprise that McDowell had bought a residence in Lake Nona, Florida.

> The weather is usually excellent on the PGA Tour, you have some excellent courses and the top players in the world play there. I enjoy the lifestyle out here. They do have more to offer, they do have TV, they do have the stars and they do have Tiger Woods. When I first went to Alabama there was a bit of a cultural change initially. But that was inevitable and it seems like such a long time ago. I'm looking forward to being back out there in the future.

McDowell, an unabashed Manchester United supporter, has read all the sports psychology books.

> I never thought much about sports psychologists. I didn't think they had much to offer. I took a certain pride in being self-maintained but when the wheels came off I had to adjust my outlook.

He is back with Dr Karl Morris, with whom he has worked intermittently.

> He is maybe the best in his field. We work well and he helps get rid of the negatives that creep into everyone's game from time to time. He helps me to be more patient and that can only be a good thing.

A back injury suffered in a car crash presented additional problems.

> For the first time in my life I had physical issues. I hurt my back and I still have problems with it today. That was a wake-up call for sure. Playing competitive golf can be such an elusive and fleeting thing. Now I know how to react to things and maintain perspective and when I work with the right people and think well, I can win golf tournaments.

The Harmons were influential in fine-tuning McDowell's swing. This was timely, as 2006 saw him miss cuts and shoot high numbers. But McDowell recognised that Harmon could only take him so far:

> I felt I was stagnating as far as my swing was concerned. That was something that needed addressing.
>   Hindsight is never wrong, of course, but taking my card on the PGA Tour was not a good decision to make in a Ryder Cup year.

Finishing runner-up to Kenny Perry in the 2005 Bay Hill Invitational in Florida (earning $500,000) emboldened the young man to try his luck in America, 'Much as I feel good about playing on that Tour, after the car crash, my game certainly wasn't ready for that kind of campaign and it really hurt my confidence.'

Another significant change was acquiring the services of Ken Conboy, an experienced and respected caddy.

> He has a keen eye for my swing and he can see when things are not just right and we can work it out together.

Caddie and player is a very important relationship and Ken has been with Paul Casey and Thomas Bjorn. More important, he has been beside them as they have come down the stretch in contention and when they've won. The experience he has gleaned with them is helping me enormously.

McDowell has also spent valuable time working with swing coach, Clive Tucker, a former tour player. Tucker explains:

Graeme's swing was too much underneath on the way back and that, coupled with a closed club face, sent his shoulders into a tilt, rather than a proper rotation. This resulted in a restricted ball flight which was too much from right to left. Pin positions located on the right side of the green were difficult to find as the landing area was restricted. Dog-leg holes from left to right were harder than they should be. When he came to me I told him there would be much repetition in his teaching in the course of the next twelve months and if he was ready to go through that, these were the changes necessary to move to the next level.

McDowell flourished under his new swing coach.

Peter Cowen, an accomplished coach, also worked on improving his short game. McDowell says:

What Peter doesn't know about pitching and chipping isn't worth knowing. He and Clive have spent time with me in that department and it has made a noticeable difference. Pin positions are now much closer to the edges, the front and back of the greens, so you need variety with your wedges and I did not have that. I have now and that puts less pressure on your iron shots. I am more confident of getting up and down.

I've elevated my game to a new level of ball-striking and thinking my way around the course. When you step up a level it takes some time to get confident at that level. I have to be comfortable with where I'm at for the wins to come. That's been the pattern since way back. It's beginning to pay dividends now.

In March 2008, McDowell won the Ballantine Championship in Korea in a playoff with India's Jeev Milah Singh. It was his third European title and his first since winning the Italian Open in 2004.

I feel like I've arrived now, as a three-time winner on the European Tour. This is the year for me. At the K Club [2006] I realised I should have been in the team. I was good enough but I wasn't there. I feel I can win multiple times this season no problem.

The Ryder Cup is a massive goal for me. Europe is the place for me to be right now trying to get on the team. I promised myself I was going to give myself every opportunity to be on Faldo's team at Valhalla. There's a lot of golf to be played this summer. I am well positioned but I can't afford a letdown.

He can certainly draw on a lot of positives from his victory in Korea. A double-bogey on the 18th hole of the second round might have derailed a lesser player. His final round with Singh developed into a two-man contest with both players trading birdies, each posting a 66 to tie on 24-under.

The drama took the two players to the third playoff hole and McDowell hit a 7-iron that he will not soon forget. If there was a defining moment for McDowell in recent times, this was surely it. Singh had fired his approach shot to within six feet. McDowell saved his best shot for last, a 179 yard 7-iron that stopped a foot from the flag, effectively clinching victory for him. 'It was definitely one of the top five shots I've ever hit, under the gun and in a playoff,'

McDowell said afterwards. 'It's just a great feeling.'

McDowell's win at the Scottish Open in early summer of 2008 ensured his place on the Ryder Cup team and gave him a terrific boost in confidence:

> We younger guys look up to Padraig, Darren and Paul. They have set a standard and they are very supportive. Padraig's win in the British Open was very inspirational. It's a victory that we can all take something from.
>
> You only have to look at the likes of Padraig and see how many times he finished second before he really broke through into the upper echelons of the best players in the world. While my career is not quite as long as Padraig's, so far it has kind of had the ups and downs that his career has maybe had. I admire his work ethic and the way he goes about things and he is certainly a guy I look towards to try and emulate a little bit.

Harrington's Ryder Cup career might have begun at Valderrama in 1997. He left it late to win his place in the 1991 team and his début could easily have been delayed until the Belfry in 2002. Notwithstanding his early cushion, McDowell is mindful that winning a place in this year's Ryder Cup team was a huge accomplishment.

The future looks bright for McDowell. He has the talent and the mindset and time is on his side. He is the best prospect of the new generation of Irish players. Make no mistake, however: if McDowell hadn't lost his PGA Tour card he would still be playing in America. That made sense financially and he will doubtless be back on the PGA Tour in the near future. In the meantime he is playing his way through the varied and far-flung locales of the European Tour:

> The one thing that the European Tour has on its side is loyalty. The players know where they come from and

there is still an underlying support and desire for the tour to do well. I will never turn my back on the European tour. There are events that I would always hope to play in. But the advantages of being on the American Tour are hard to resist.

> That said, it is a solitary existence. The European Tour is much more of a unit. We all seem to be on the same flights and many of the players stay in the same hotels. We often eat together and have a laugh. In America it's all a little individual but I will go back and play there. You really have to be up there in the world rankings to play both Tours, so that's in the future.

With the Ryder Cup in mind, McDowell moved back to his roots in Portrush. He is under the management of Conor Ridge of Horizon Sports Management and appears to have a more positive outlook and clearer direction.

> Now I'm back home, I can live a normal life, see my friends and family when I want to and it's easier for them to see me. I can go to my local and have a couple of pints of Guinness and generally get away from life on tour. I have a sound base and I'm much more relaxed.

McDowell smiles when reminded that Harrington turned pro as a twenty-four-year-old in 1995 and won the Spanish Open in his first season as a pro. Harrington waited for five years until his second Tour victory. He was twenty-eight when he made his Ryder Cup début in 1999. Says McDowell:

> I have a strong team around me, a team I have total trust in. I think I have made mainly the right moves, the moves I needed to make. But I'm under no illusions. I have to continue to work hard and I'm ready for that challenge.

DAMIEN MCGRANE

Damien McGrane may have been the least known of the 2008 Ryder Cup contenders. In the golfing world guys like him are called journeymen, a pejorative and inappropriate term. They go about their business unfussily and largely below the radar. They are to be found on all the Tours. Many are content to remain in that comfortable, anonymous category.

Every swing on the professional tours represents thousands if not hundreds of thousands of pounds, euros, dollars. Take away the glamour of the opulent clubhouses, the range balls new and shiny and what are left are the hardest and fastest greens in the world, the highest and toughest roughs. The immaculate fairways are narrower than at any other time of the year.

Brad Faxon (US), regarded by many as one of the game's best putters, adds some perspective:

> The good club players and good amateurs don't understand the difference. Good players I play with when I'm home say, 'You know, I hit it as far as you and as close as you a lot of the time. I must be close.' They might shoot even par and I might shoot one-under when we're out playing a casual round at home but they don't realise how different it is out there.
>
> They can't imagine hitting a perfect 9-iron from a perfect lie and having the ball bounce over the back of the green, or hitting what they think as a perfect putt and having it roll off the green and into a bunker. Those are the conditions we find every week on the Tour. I do have a problem with scribes who refer to these professionals as journeymen. It connotes something lesser, something inadequate, when being out there in the first place is all one needs to know. The guys on the Tour know this and respect all their opponents.

It is possible to become very wealthy and never win a tournament, especially on the PGA Tour. The European Tour may not be quite as lucrative but it is worth noting that in 2007, the 100th player on the Order of Merit earned €263,332, not including endorsements. Even allowing for travel, hotel and caddie expenses, this is a significant income.

McGrane is unassuming to the point of self-disparagement. This self-assessment is based on what has been a long road to success, with several trips to Q School, chasing a dream that he knew was attainable but seemed more remote with every year on tour. He describes himself as an ordinary man but it is clear that he is a well-rounded and insightful individual.

Several high-profile professional golfers pay big money to sports psychologists in order to gain the balance and perspective that McGrane always had. McGrane doesn't have to be reminded of what matters in the real world; no one has to advise him to get out of his own way as he struggles with his game.

In April 2008, the Kells native won the Volvo China Open in Beijing by nine strokes. This was his maiden victory on the European Tour and he was so far ahead of the field in the final round that the win was almost anti-climactic. The win gave him a handsome pay cheque of €230,121, pushing him to a career-high sixth position in the Order of Merit.

The win capped a steady progression that began last November and carried over to the new year when he finished second in the Indian Masters in Delhi in February and sixth in the Portuguese Open in April. It was a win that was greeted warmly by his fellow Irish players and his many Irish supporters.

He got hundreds of messages from Wexford GC, where he became club professional in 1997. These were people he knew as well as his next-door neighbour, who texted him every day on his way to winning. He left Wexford over four years ago but his popularity there endures.

He fully understands the implications of his first win. It is uncommon to win a first title at the age of thirty-seven. It is even more uncommon to do it after coming from what he refers to as the very bottom. Headfort members in Kells (the family club), watched him since he was a child starting out. They knew about his ambitions and, like the members at Wexford, their support through the years was unstinting. They rightly take considerable pride in his achievement.

McGrane fashioned his win in Irish conditions of heavy rain. His excellent short game enabled him to get up and down with relative ease. He averaged twenty-four putts per round and 1.66 in putts per green hit in regulation. With a short game that was razor-sharp, McGrane didn't have to do anything special to win in a hack.

Starting from the bottom for McGrane meant coming through the ranks of the Irish amateur system. McGrane captured the Irish Boys' title at Birr GC in 1988, three strokes ahead of Padraig Harrington. Two years later McGrane lost out to Mark Gannon at the 19th hole in the third round of the Irish Close at Baltray.

McGrane doesn't put himself in the same category as Clarke, Harrington or McGinley. That's not to say he doesn't believe in himself. He always knew that what he had in his head was good enough if he could get it on to the golf course. Moreover, he didn't need a Bob Rotella to tell him what he already knew. McGrane is self-maintained and doesn't sweat the technical side of things. He has stayed within his own certainties.

For two years or more he was saying that a win was close, that he had what it takes. Many professional golfers delude themselves in this area and enter a twilight of denial. In truth, they will never win anything. McGrane was perhaps becoming a bit frustrated that success was so close. But he understands that golf is a game that doesn't owe anybody anything.

In the meantime he got to play with Tiger Woods in the final two rounds of the Dubai Desert Classic. He was asked what he had in common with Woods and told a battery of journalists: 'I think we had dinner in the same restaurant the other night. That's about it.' Pressed further, he added:

He has his game and I have my game and I try to do the best with what I have. This is what it's about, isn't it? This is why we practise so hard and work continuously to improve what we do.

Everybody would like to play with Tiger. We want to be out there competing with the best players in the world but it's important to stay focused on your own game, which is what I try to do. I wouldn't feel intimidated by any playing partner and I did okay.

He finished the third round level with Woods on 209 but on the final day Woods shot a 65 and McGrane slipped out of contention.

He had his sights on a Ryder Cup place and he knew another win might close the deal for him on that. Having won once, he wanted to become a serious contender in all events. Whether he can build on this win remains to be seen; he will not get carried away. 'Good things will happen only if I continue to play well.'

He did not make the 2008 Ryder Cup team but he is a likely contender for the 2010 competition. 'The Ryder Cup is the perfect stage for the sub-elite player like McGrane to rise to the occasion and take out the bigger names,' says Peter Oosterhuis, a man uniquely qualified to make this statement.

RORY MCILROY: A CAUTIONARY TALE

I am backing myself to do well and I would be disappointed if at the end of 2008 if I haven't won a tournament. I will be going out with the mindset that I am as good if not better than all these guys out here and that's the mindset you have to adopt – that I am good enough to win out here. That's all I am thinking about.

The history of the Irish and the Ryder Cup is noteworthy for brief moments of glory followed by decline and mediocrity. In many cases the fall-off was caused by injury. Philip Walton and Ronan Rafferty are the most striking examples of the peaks and valleys of professional golf. And while we are eager to embrace the talent of Rory McIlroy, we need to temper our expectations. Irish and European golf stand to benefit hugely if the enthusiastic and brash youngster goes on to early and sustained success.

McIlroy's talent was evident from a very young age. He began to attract national attention after his performance in the 2004 West of Ireland Amateur Golf Championship. When he was fourteen, spectators were privileged to see a precocious yet vulnerable talent hit eight birdies in sixteen holes, defeating Pat Murray, the veteran Irish international. In 2005 McIlroy won the 'West' at the age of fifteen, the youngest ever winner, beating the record set by legendary Cecil Ewing in 1930 at the age of seventeen.

Michael Bannon was one of the key people in the development of McIlroy from the beginning. Bannon, the Bangor Club PGA professional, has watched the youngster since he was four.

> By the time he was eight or nine he had the ability to play a whole array of shots. He showed a great feel for the game as a kid and you cannot teach that. I began working with him in earnest around that time and much of the work on developing and grooving his swing was done in the early years. Even as a kid, when he played in under-age events in America, he stood out.

Bannon has seen more than a few talented players come through with varying degrees of success. He turned pro in 1981, a year after he lost the final of the Irish Amateur Close Championship to Ronan Rafferty. Among these were Rafferty, Walton, Darren Clarke and Raymie Burns. Bannon sees McIlroy as being 'in the same mould as Seve and Sergio Garcia'.

Many shrewd observers have made similar comments. There is much to admire in McIlroy's game. Bannon adds:

Rory has got great flair and perhaps his greatest asset is his balance throughout the swing. All his position and power moves are excellent. We've developed a great relationship and dynamic down the years. It's a two-way thing. I always ask him now how he feels about any moves we consider making but really it's down to fine-tuning at this stage when we meet.

McIlroy's talent was beamed to a global audience at the 2007 Open. The youngster captured not only the amateur medal but the admiration of golf fans everywhere. He was truly on his way. As a child, McIlroy idolised Nick Faldo, this year's Ryder Cup captain. Faldo has seen the young man close-up on several occasions.

He's got that self-belief and swagger. That's going to be very important to him. Every part of his game is there.

Faldo advises caution at this point. He should know, having turned pro early and gone out on Tour at nineteen. He was twenty when he made it on to the Ryder Cup team. 'You have to have serious belief in yourself when going out on Tour. I say give him a couple of years. You can't put that pressure on anybody. Let's see what happens.'

McIlroy turned professional in September 2007 and was signed on by IMS Group. His initial £1 million contract was also laden with achievement incentives. Clarke, McDowell and McGinley are also managed by IMS and Clarke was influential in having the youngster sign with the group. He also became Tour pro for Lough Erne Golf Resort in Hollywood, County Fermanagh. Under the shrewd guidance of Chubby Chandler, McIlroy assembled an impressive support group.

He made headlines almost immediately with a whirlwind start to his pro career. He finished third in his second European Tour event. Chubby Chandler beamed:

I knew he was good but I had no idea hew was that good. It was just staggering to watch him close up. I have never in professional golf come across an eighteen-year-old as gifted as him. I didn't see Tiger at that age but I cannot imagine anyone being as good as Rory. He has an awful lot of game and an astonishing temperament.

Paul Lawrie, former Open champion, partnered McIlroy on his pro début:

There is nothing he can't do. He is going to be a hell of a player. He doesn't get down on himself. That was the most impressive thing – he has a variety of shots. He shapes the ball both ways depending on where the flag is. Sometimes he will put a lot of spin on it and other times he lets it run up.

Padraig Harrington is in a unique position to observe and comment on the progress of the young professional:

His performance initially ensured that his transition from amateur to professional ranks has been really smooth. So much in professional golf hinges on the start that you make. He won't be without competitive golf, having taken the direct route by securing his card early. He's up and running and he's found no difference between amateur and professional golf and that's really great. It's brilliant for him and fantastic for Irish golf.

McIlroy characteristically made known his intentions early in 2008. His sights were set on winning tournaments and playing Ryder Cup:

If I could win soon it is going to get me well up the points list and if that happens, there's a big possibility of breaking into the team. It's certainly feasible and it's not unrealistic setting that as a goal. It is well within my capability and if I didn't have that belief I'd be wasting my time out here.

He speaks with assurance and self-confidence and is comfortable in the professional environment. He has been around the pro game since his very early days and there is no intimidation factor. McIlroy is also a vindication of the nurturing policy of the Golfing Union of Ireland. 'I have travelled all over the world at their expense and they have been fantastic,' he says.

The praise is well-merited and it is gratifying to see an Irish sporting organisation getting the success it deserves. McIlroy is not yet the finished product; at this point he may well be a can't-miss prospect. He is mindful of the journey ahead: 'Half the battle out here is feeling comfortable in your new environment and I've heard people say that I have a old head on young shoulders and I agree with that totally.'

The transition to full-time touring professional is fraught with unexpected obstacles, surprises, setbacks and many times a loss in form. 'It's been a whirlwind twelve months for me and I am just trying to take it all in my stride. You can't really predict what's going to happen but I will continue to work hard and be dedicated.'

The young Hollywood star is beginning to realise that what came easily to him in the amateur game is considerably more difficult to achieve in the professional ranks. Despite his rapid start as a professional, McIlroy has discovered that he has much to learn before he can contend for victory on a consistent basis. All the self-belief in the world is not enough on its own. To this point in his career, McIlroy has learnt how to win. How he deals with losing and missing cuts may be his greatest challenge.

'Whenever I wasn't in contention in an amateur tournament, I didn't really care. I wasn't losing anything,' he said before finishing in fifteenth position in the Estoril Portuguese Open:

But here you are losing money, losing points, losing rankings. So you have to try and give 100 percent and finish the best you can. If I was running fifteenth in an amateur event I wouldn't let that bother me but here you have to try and get the best of every week.

He is also fully cognisant that there are no short-cuts to success. 'Very few people have come from where I have come from and gone straight to the top of the professional game. You just have to be patient and bide your time.'

All the indications pointed to a keener than ever battle for European places. From an Irish perspective, the only certainties seemed to be Harrington and Clarke.

McIlroy was in contention for a place and capable of securing one but his game faltered as the season progressed. He didn't emerge from the chasing pack in the little time that remained and he didn't make the Ryder Cup team.

18

Remembering to Forget

It's always been said you have to be really smart or
really dumb to play golf but nothing in between. You
have to be very smart to focus or just be an airhead to
be out here and not worrying too much.

Jerry Pate, speaking at the 2008 Liberty Mutual
Legends of Golf, Savannah, Georgia

Golf today is not the same game that it was thirty, twenty or even ten
years ago. The financial rewards are a lot greater and the competition
is much deeper. The developments in equipment technology have
levelled the playing field and there is increasing parity in the talent
level among the professional ranks.

More and more there is an emphasis on physical and mental
strength. The line between success and failure is so minute that
players will go to great lengths to maximise their opportunities.
Fitness trailers, mental coaches and nutrition specialists are part and
parcel of the modern game.

Physical strength can be attained and the basics of the game
can be learned; it seems that the mental side of the game is the
great unknown. It's invisible and unquantifiable, hence the presence
of outside assistance – mind coaches, mental gurus and sports
psychologists, with varying levels of credibility.

There are conflicting opinions about the value of these mental
gurus, many of whom have never picked up a golf club or hit a ball.
Says David Feherty:

In my day we didn't have fitness trailers. We were lucky to have trailers. We did sit-downs instead of sit-ups and Jack Daniels was a cure-all for every known demon. It was a bit like sex in Ireland; we didn't know a lot of these mental conditions even existed. Maybe they didn't. You sometimes felt off-colour after the night before but that was easily fixed and you could play away once the hands stopped shaking. I played a lot of excellent golf in those circumstances...as far as I can remember.

The mental men are here to stay. If players feel that these guys are helping them, who can argue with that? You should go ask J.D. [John Daly] what he thinks about physical and mental fitness.

American golfer John Daly is the antithesis of the modern golfer. The two-time Major winner is the beer-chugging, smoking man's hero. He does not have a mental coach:

I got enough alimony payments to make as it is so why should I waste my money on some dude that's never played the frickin game. Hey, if it works for guys go for it. I don't take kindly to instruction of any kind. I like to fix things for myself and why fix something that's not broken?

I would say the number 1 obstacle to hitting a good golf shot is your head. Not moving it or anything. Using it. That's the truth, bro. You gotta get your head out of the game. With all the thinking going on, you wonder why every swing isn't messed up. The short answer is: don't think. Sounds easy but it's not. I do all my thinking on the driving range. When I step up to hit the ball my mind is blank. See, I already know what I am going to do before I address the ball. It's then a case of hitting the damned thing.

Another irritation is the amount of time players spend on the driving range before and after playing a competitive round. I never practise the day of a tournament. All I do is get ready to play, man. To me the only reason to go to the range before going out to play is to loosen up, not to practise.

Jack Nicklaus once said that if he hit a dozen good shots in a row he'd stop right there and head on over to the first tee. He said he didn't want to waste any good shots at the range; he wanted to save them all for when they counted. If that's good enough for Jack Nicklaus, it's good enough for me.

You won't find me hanging around the driving range after a round, especially after a bad round. I want to get the hell out of Dodge pron to, get my butt back on the bus and have a few coldies. A lot of the guys on the Tour don't agree with that but, hey, it's my way of doing things.

And you know something else? Did Jack, Arnie, Trevino or any of those guys have mental coaches? Like hell they did. And don't tell me they didn't have competition and pressure. Yeah, competion is deeper now blah, blah, blah, but those guys played against one another all the time and they didn't have it as easy as we are led to believe.

For all his seeming flippancy, there is merit to what Daly is saying. Yet professional golf is crowded with hugely talented players who never manage to exploit their potential fully. It seems their inability to manage and control their thoughts, temper tantrums and emotions compromises their capacity to 'close the deal on a Sunday'.

How how does Tiger Woods, the world number 1, deal with the mental aspect of the game? His comments in the 2006 Buick interview are valuable. Asked about how his mental game had matured over the years he replied:

Oh, a lot. It's just experience. I've put myself in so many different scenarios and have been successful and have failed and I've had to learn from both. Why did I fail? Well, because of this. Why did I succeed? Well because of this. You have to analyse, you have to be critical and you have to understand that you have to take hard looks at yourself.

Over the years I've done that and I think that's one of the reasons why I've been able to keep progressing through the years. Trust me, it's not always easy but my father always harped on me, always be honest with yourself, true to yourself, look yourself in the mirror and be honest. Some days are tougher than others. When you know you've absolutely messed up, you have to admit it and move on and learn and apply. And I've done that.

PGATour.com

At the 2006 Ryder Cup all the top golf coaches were somewhere in the vicinity of the K Club. Bob Rotella was there to talk to his players, including Padraig Harrington. Ian Woosnam the European captain, called in new-wave mentalist Jamil Qureshi to lighten the mood in the European camp.

Quereshi, a former Warwickshire cricketer, is also a hypnotist and mental coach to some of the game's top players, including Lee Westwood and Thomas Bjorn. He was the official mental coach to the team and believes that golfers need to be themselves on the course and not get too caught up with introspection.

He had the players and their wives in stitches, using humour to quell anxiety. 'It was a terrific bonding session,' he said, 'and the whole mood of the evening was tremendously positive.' He drew caricatures of Colin Montgomerie with an Afro; he nicked a watch from assistant captain Peter Baker. The players were certainly relaxed.

He also read Des Smyth's mind, guessing the headline in a

magazine that Smyth picked up and opened at random. 'He was an absolute scream,' Smyth said. 'He took the mickey out of all the lads and it was great fun. It was just amazing and great craic.'

There are countless mind doctors on the Tour who spend a lot of time dressing up conventional wisdom and complicating common-sense. Butch Harmon, one of the world's most reputable swing coaches, is not impressed:

> They may not be doing any harm but I fail to see what good they are doing.
>
> When a player is facing a crucial shot and the red dot [camera] is trained on him, alone, watched by millions all over the world, where is the mental coach then? He's like the rest of us, just a passive observer. Look, the top players get it done anyway. They always have and they always will. But I see more and more guys using them and all I can say is: it's your money, pal.

The name of the game for mind coaches is success – or perceived success. If they don't get their player to play better they're gone. Many players have tried several coaches, hoping to find the one who will unlock the secret and impart the wisdom.

There is an increasing concern that sports psychology is failing not only golfers but athletes in general. The textbooks in sports psychology are tending toward extremely superficial work. There is virtually no discussion about the actual dynamics inside the minds of golfers.

There are lots of suppressive techniques on how to manage anxiety, anger or lack of focus. There is no commentary on typical diagnosis of golfers and the necessary psychotherapy, or the possibility that their anxieties may be symptomatic of something deeper and more troubling. There is an assumption (or denial) that golfers have a premium on mental stability and just need a pep talk and all is better.

Golf is no place to have anxiety. Golfers are just like you and me. They have their neurosis, anxieties, depression and personality problems. There are many who ought to be offered some real diagnosis, real support, real therapy and worthwhile insight into what is causing them such grief. If sports psychology fails to address this it will be in danger of becoming a joke.

There is a culture of learned helplessness prevalent among golfers and presence of the mental coaches confirms this. Does this dependency pave the way for drug use? The use of steroids to recover faster from injuries comes immediately to mind.

David Feherty has his own views on this and they are relevant because he was a spectacular functioning alcoholic before he learned that he was, in fact, suffering from clinical depression:

> I survived it because of the understanding and support of my wife Anita, my children and close friends. Sam Torrance and his wife knew about my condition from the beginning and apart from family, I owe them more than I can say. Actually, Sam *is* family.
>
> Let me tell you something: if they find a drug that will improve your golf, I will be pissed! Because I tried to find it for twenty years and I couldn't find one that worked. And I tried them all.

19

Faldo's Follies: Valhalla 2008

USA: 16½ Europe 11½

History will judge Nick Faldo as Ryder Cup captain
with one question: did he win or lose?

Padraig Harrington

Captain Cock-Up Does It Again
Daily Mail headline, 21 September 2008

Nick Faldo forgets the captain's golden rule – lose and
it's all your fault.

Daily Mirror, 22 September 2008

In Valhalla, in September 2008, the US team played inspired golf to
recover the Ryder Cup for the first time since 1999. The defeat of
Europe was comprehensive and the margin of victory the highest
since 1981. History will remember Nick Faldo as the captain who
lost the Ryder Cup. The victory of the Americans will define his
captaincy, whether this is reasonable or not. Faldo was never all that
popular in his prime, notwithstanding his remarkable successes.
Defeat at Valhalla brought his detractors out in force.

It mystified many that Faldo omitted Darren Clarke, while the
selection of Ian Poulter seemed indefensible as the Englishman
hadn't bothered to try and play his way on to the team at Gleneagles.
Irish professional Gary Murphy says:

We were all surprised. Darren looked like a perfect fit and looked like he would play well. And he's been there before. It was a poor decision. I played with him at Gleneagles on Sunday. It was the best ball-striking I've seen on Tour this year, and I've played with Sergio [García]. Darren won twice this year; he supports the European Tour whereas Poulter and Casey don't. It's a no-brainer. Given that he's played in five Ryder Cups, that surely counts.

Wild-cards should be all about who'se going to help the team with regard to pairings. [Faldo] hasn't really done that. He's just gone down the rankings list. He's spoken about stats. Who cares about stats? Results are the only stats that matter, not how you drive or how you putt.

Des Smyth was equally perplexed: 'Darren seemed the logical choice. He was playing well and he had momentum.'

Clarke accepted his omission with his customary dignity and wished the team well. There is an argument that the 2008 European team began to unravel because of Faldo's surprise picks. That may well be but both Poulter and Casey justified their inclusion by playing superb golf.

So, David, what's your take on this?

Oddly enough, I happen to know that it was a decision Faldo agonised over. It really bothered him to leave the big lad [Clarke] out.

I wasn't too thrilled either. I think he took Poulter because of his couldn't–give-a-fuck attitude about whether they're American or not. Plus, you can pair Westwood with anyone. Faldo was on a hiding to nothing. Why should we be surprised that the Yanks beat us on their home turf with a loud but well-behaved crowd? You can blame it on the environment, on the economy, or maybe because Faldo is a lifelong Leeds United supporter. What an affliction!

There was superb golf out there but the Americans played out of their skins and it seemed like all their putts were going in. How can you prepare for that? Of course it stings to be on the losing end. But I was proud of Jimenez when he picked up Furyk's ball and conceded the match that gave them the Cup. There was a quiet dignity about it, an admission: fair play; you beat us this time'

Why did Europe lose the Ryder Cup in Valhalla and can we justifiably castigate captain Nick Faldo?

In pre-Ryder Cup interviews, Faldo made some peculiar comments. There was a sense of distance and aloofness about him even at this year's Masters:

What I've said to them (the players) is, 'You talk to me. If you want anything from me, you call me.' I am very accessible…I am not going to start calling guys asking, 'What do you need?'…If you want me, you call me. If I don't hear from them I'm happy.

That may not have been what the players wanted to hear, or were used to hearing from previous captains. Perhaps Faldo felt he was accessible but the rookies under consideration, who knew him only by his playing reputation, never felt comfortable with this.

Hopefully everybody will arrive and be super-confident and we can all keep riding the waves. You have to duck and dive a bit. So much of what we have to deal with is going to be about the atmosphere…I'm going to do team meetings a bit different from the way they have been done before…

We will decide what emotional state we want to

project. We'll get the balance right. But I think we'll pay more attention to detail than them. The Americans have the attitude that they are all great players and they plonk them in and see what happens.

The toughest thing in the Ryder Cup is asking four players to sit out for a reason. They won't just be told they are dropped. It will be discussed by everyone. Honesty is really important.

Regarding pressure situations I'd rather a guy was playing good on Sunday and very confident. Hopefully I can tell if someone has got it inside them to deal with those pressure situations. I think I can do that.

These comments point to a man out of touch both with his players and with the responsibilities of a Ryder Cup captain. They are cliché-ridden and hollow. Faldo was found wanting even before the matches began.

Faldo's speech at the opening ceremony was an embarrassment. One can forgive him for getting Henrik Stenson's name wrong – 'Denmark's Soren Stenson' – while introducing the players, but having a man who is a professional golf analyst attributing this gaffe to nerves is hardly convincing.

When Sam Torrance was captain he went to enormous lengths to hit the right note in the lead-up to the Cup. He practiced his opening speech over and over and came across as being natural, passionate – certainly inoffensive. Torrance understood the value of setting the right tone when it mattered most. Faldo was notably out of tune and perhaps out of touch.

No one can say what effect any of this had on the outcome. Had Europe retained the Cup, there would scarcely be a reference to the opening formalities. The perennial problem for Faldo is that he sets himself up, often unwittingly, as an easy target, to be shot at when the occasion arises. His role as captain will be picked apart and debated until the next Ryder Cup in 2010 and beyond.

GRAEME MCDOWELL

Graeme McDowell will have mixed feelings about his first Ryder Cup. He looked very composed and he made a considerable contribution. It was an auspicious début and he should be a fixture in future European teams. He silenced many of his critics, not for the first time:

> It was brilliant, except for the result. An amazing experience really, a roller-coaster of emotions. You read about all the other guys who went through this and then you're out there in the thick of it. Nick is obviously going to be criticised for the way he put his team out on Sunday but I don't think any criticism of the line-up is warranted. Captains live and die by their decisions. Nick could have been a hero with that line-up today. He is going to turn out the villain...unnecessarily.

McDowell believes that the cup was lost when the US took the opening day foursome session 3-1 and maintained their lead in the afternoon fourballs. The Americans enjoyed their best opening day at a Ryder Cup since 1979.

> We were three back after the first day. Myself and Padraig had played fantastic golf against Mickelson and Kim in the fourballs and got beaten. To get nothing from a game like that was tough. It seemed like they were getting the half-points. Even on Saturday, when I thought we dominated play, we didn't get much reward for it and pulled only one point back.
>
> It seemed like they were getting up and down on the last day. It was all the halves. It's amazing the difference just one point can make. To me as a Ryder Cup rookie, I thought two points (on Sunday) was nothing but for some reason when you get out there, it's a lot to catch up on. So, like I say, I think it was lost on Friday.

Speaking a few days after the match McDowell added:

> I was on the 16th fairway in the ninth match and I
> realised I was on the losing side. When the noise came
> reverberating back to me and we lost, that was a huge
> deflation.
>
> You always picture what the Sunday singles are
> going to look like but that was certainly not the script I
> had read so it was hugely deflating. If we were going to
> win, it was going to be close and those last four games
> were going to be huge. In hindsight you wish you had
> started them at the front...but we were conscious
> that the last four or five matches were important and
> Harrington was a big believer in that.

Even though Faldo insisted that there was no panic, his
demeanour indicated otherwise. He was shaken and the television
cameras captured a haunted look. Tony Jacklin was the first to see it
all beginning to unravel. During the Friday morning play he vented
his displeasure on Skysport: 'He has to put his head on the pillow
and sleep comfortably long after this match is finished...' said the
former captain, perhaps a little harshly

Peter Oosterhuis, who had told us to expect the unexpected, was
unsettled by Faldo's demeanour. 'He looks about a hundred years
older than when I played with him in 1977,' he said. Faldo benched
his two most accomplished Ryder cuppers, Westwood and García,
for the Saturday-morning foursomes. They were 8-0-1 in foursomes
play.

But the Europeans rallied, taking 2½ points in the session to
close the deficit, and set up an afternoon of classic Ryder Cup golf.
Three of the matches went to the 18th hole. The final hour of play
was so tense that the American captain Paul Azinger admitted that
he was experiencing stomach cramps.

The heaviest criticism was of Faldo's Sunday line-up. With the
Americans heading into the singles matches leading 9-7, it was

imperative to get back on even terms and not lose further ground. The first slot in Sunday's singles is usually reserved for the team's emotional leader and Faldo sent out García against Kim.

García was never a factor as Kim made 7 birdies over the first 13 holes, giving the Spaniard a 5-4 drubbing. When Kenny Perry, the forty-eight-year-old from Kentucky, secured another point, beating Stenson 3 and 2, the Americans were four points ahead and on their way to victory.

Putting the world's hottest golfer, Padraig Harrington, out last was a mistake. Holding back Lee Westwood and Ian Poulter compounded the error. The efforts of Harrington and Westwood were made irrelevant by the early results. The Americans won by five points but the score is deceptive. There was a period in the Sunday singles when the Europeans looked like they were going to turn the match around. But this rally fizzled out. There was simply too much ground to make up.

PADRAIG HARRINGTON

It was a disappointing Ryder Cup for the three-time Major winner. Half a point seems a meagre return for a player of his stature after an equally disappointing half-point at the K Club in 2006. Harrington was clearly not at his best in Valhalla; he was jaded, a spent force, and might not have fared much better against Kim had he gone out first. But his stature demanded that he should be the first European out.

After securing his second Major of the year, Harrington had one week off before heading back Stateside for a three-week campaign in the FEDEX Cup. After celebrating his thirty-seventh birthday in Ireland, it was on to Valhalla.:

> I'm happy I didn't leave any stone unturned in terms of trying but I just didn't have it this week. I'm tired.
>
> My preparation was not right coming into the Ryder Cup and it showed up 100 percent this week. How well I perform on any given week depends on my preparation and because of scheduling and things

like that it just wasn't right this time. That's just the way things went. Obviously, I haven't been right since winning those two [Majors] in the middle of summer.

This fatigue was inevitable. Harrington is now among the elite of world golf and in the absence of Tiger Woods, might reasonably be regarded as the best player in the world. He has set standards for himself and continues to raise them. He seems very likely to win more Majors in the next few years and his Ryder Cup performance may continue to suffer as a result.

Jack Nicklaus knows exactly what Harrington is dealing with:

> I remember what it was like as a Ryder Cup player. Sure, it was a great honour to make the team and to represent my country but frankly, when the matches rolled around in September, I was nearly golfed out. I'm sure Padraig gears all his preparation around the Majors. There is massive pressure right there.
>
> Now that he has started winning them it's easy to understand that his mindset for the Ryder Cup would necessarily change. Tiger has the same issues. I never played my best in the Ryder Cup. After going at maximum intensity for the four Majors it's just not possible to maintain that focus and get up for the Ryder Cup. If that's the trade-off for winning the Majors, so be it.

Des Smyth watched all the matches from his home in Drogheda. I will leave the last word in the book to this gentleman of golf:

> It was a great contest. You could easily point fingers and play the blame game but you have to hand it to the Yanks. They were brilliant and they deserved the victory, no question.
>
> Yes, I was unhappy that Darren wasn't selected but

you'll have controversial decisions in every Ryder Cup. I would question Faldo's line-up on Sunday. I believe you put your best players out, especially if you are behind, but he's the captain and that's his call. It was closer than the score suggests and it was great to see McDowell doing the business.

I was certain that Europe would win and I also felt that Darren would be in the line-up. But we have a lot of talent in Ireland now and we can look to the future with great expectations. We certainly haven't seen the last of Clarke or Paul (McGinley), Padraig or Graeme.

We'll be in there and then we have the prospect of the youngster (Rory McIlroy) coming through.